The Black Economy

Arnold Heertje became Professor of Economics at the University of Amsterdam in 1964. He has developed his interests to encompass economic issues on an international scale and has lectured in many countries. Professor Heertje has an extensive list of English-language publications to his name including the textbooks *Economics and Technical Change* and *Basic Economics*.

Margaret Allen has spent many years in journalism on the *Investors Chronicle*, the *Economist*, the *Evening Standard* and *The Times* where she was until recently features editor. She is now a full-time writer and is author of *The Money Book* and *A Guide to Insurance*, both published in Pan Books.

Harry Cohen is an economist and researcher.

Arnold Heertje,
Margaret Allen and
Harry Cohen

The Black Economy

A Pan Original
Pan Books London and Sydney

The following sources are referred to in the text:

p. 62   *The Economics of Avoidance/Evasion*, Institute of Economic Affairs, 1979.

p. 81   Mars and Nicod: Centre for Occupational and Community Research, Middlesex Polytechnic.

p. 107   Frey and Wech: Institute for Empirical and Economic Research, University of Zurich.

p. 108   E. L. Feige: *Challenge*, November/December 1979.

p. 114   Seminar, 'The Hidden Economy', March 1980: Outer Circle Policy Unit.

p. 119   *Economic Trends*, HMSO, February 1980.

p. 125   M. O'Higgins, Measuring the Hidden Economy: A Review of Evidence and Methodologies, Outer Circle Policy Unit, July 1980.

p. 126   E. L. Feige: *Journal of Economic Affairs*, July 1981.

p. 129   J. Ditton: *Assessment*, September 1981.

First published in Great Britain 1982 by Pan Books Ltd,
Cavaye Place, London SW10 9PG
This edition is a translated and revised version of
Het Officieuze Circuit
by A. Heertje and H. Cohen, published 1980 by
Uitgeverij Het Spectrum
of Utrecht and Antwerp
© De Echte Kern and Margaret Allen 1982
ISBN 0 330 26765 5
Printed and bound in Great Britain by
Hunt Barnard Ltd, Aylesbury, Bucks

Contents

1 It's a universal problem

One day in the summer of 1980, the *International Herald Tribune* carried an article on the United States balance of payments. In the course of it, the author revealed that the discrepancy of nearly $25,000 million it showed was a mystery to laymen and experts alike. That discrepancy and other transactions missing from the official figures are the subject of this book.

A country's balance of payments over a year is a summary of all the economic transactions concluded with other countries in that year and includes an item at the end known as the balancing or residual item. This is a kind of dustbin for errors and omissions in the records and for miscellaneous transactions that are difficult to classify under other headings. When it is very large, something must be wrong. In the case of the USA nearly $25,000 million had reached the country during 1979 and had subsequently completely disappeared. The *Tribune* article mentioned the following possible reasons for this large discrepancy:

- that in the case of some large sums of money reaching the country from abroad, neither their origin nor destination was known;
- that some money reached the country through figureheads, relatives and secret bank accounts, and was not officially recorded;
- that the authorities did and do not always know the level of Arab buying of US bonds;
- that US exporters invoiced foreign buyers for more

than the value of the goods, and so the foreigners in question could invest secretly in the USA. If this is the case then true exports would be less than the figures showed;
- that in some countries, the central bank might not have supplied accurate information about the amount of dollars it held;
- that the compilers of the figures made some monumental mistakes; say, putting an item expressed in Japanese yen in the column for items expressed in dollars.

When there is money which cannot be reconciled with the official transactions unofficial transactions must be assumed to take place to make the figures tally. There are also transactions of which there is absolutely no trace in the official figures (besides the $25,000 million which is known to have been missing in the USA in 1979, there may have been further discrepancies, of which there is no knowledge at all). These huge discrepancies in the USA's budget are a representative example of a problem which, because of its widespread occurrence, should be treated as an international one. However, we shall be concentrating on the British case, where estimates of the unofficial economy vary between two per cent and 15½ per cent of the whole; even the higher figure may be an underestimate, as we will see.

In the American case, the discrepancy which arose was not due entirely to unlawful transactions, but also to economic activities covering a wide spectrum from the absolutely legal to the illegal, through a vast grey area. We shall therefore be dealing not only with what is now commonly called 'black' money and the illegal economy, but also with those distortions in the economy that do not necessarily contravene the law. Their common feature is that they form the unofficial economy where, as in the official economy, there are goods and services on one side and payments on the other. The unofficial economy is that part of the total economy which does not show up in the official figures. It may also be known as the informal, irregular, secondary, alternative, hidden, twilight, second or underground economy, but the word 'unofficial' seems best to describe the transactions in question, which have to be added to the official ones to get the full economic picture, or show a nation's real state of economic affairs.

Britain's economic policy-making is at present based entirely on the official economic figures; the unofficial economy is taken into account only when the subject of 'black' money hits the newspaper headlines. A sober account of what is happening below the surface of official economy is clearly needed.

Money earned but not declared for tax purposes may not exist for the tax man, but it is just as real as 'white' money for the economist, in its effects on national income and income distribution. We shall discuss how black money materializes, how it is 'laundered' (that is, finds its way back into official money circulation), and what it means for the national economy.

Besides this illegal side, the unofficial economy also has a grey and even a white side. Hidden employment is one example. It has been recognized in Britain and other developed countries that the unemployment picture is distorted by the rules for the disabled. Not counted officially among the unemployed are those people who, after receiving sickness benefits for six months, are still too incapacitated to work either permanently or periodically for medical, psychological or social reasons, and are moved on to other forms of benefit. If the beneficiaries of state disablement insurance schemes were included in the unemployment figures, these figures would be correspondingly higher. At the same time, of course, some people drawing disablement benefits may well be 'moonlighting' without the knowledge of the authorities – thus counterbalancing hidden unemployment with hidden employment.

In the case of production, too, there is a difference between the reality and official figures. Housework in one's own home, which may be called production, is one case; housework done for others which may not appear in official figures, hidden production, is another.

A third case can arise: anyone earning less than £27 a week, £117 a month or £1,404 a year in Britain need not pay national insurance contributions. This has temporary benefits (though it puts people outside the benefits available under the social security system: for example, sickness benefits, unemployment pay and pensions); take-home pay is higher and the employer, too, benefits from not having to pay his part of the national insurance contribution. This means that a further large number of people's earnings are excluded from the official figures.

Probably the biggest section of the economic population 'missing' in this way is the army of housewives who work in other people's homes. Many of these people do one or two jobs and it is not difficult for their weekly wages to top £27, when they should pay NI contributions with the first employer in the week paying the employer's contribution. If it was suggested to housewives that they should be paying contributions and reporting their wages through their husbands to the taxman, most would be genuinely astonished.

Other kinds of hidden production arise when people make reciprocal arrangements with one another to provide services. Mutual babysitting, taking phone messages, giving lifts in cars, swapping garden produce and assisting on do-it-yourself projects in the home can all be regarded as payments in kind. So, too, is the work done in the home: looking after the children, cooking or doing housework. This is a full-time job for many women – and some men. The fact that one may enjoy the task does not make it any the less genuine work (hence the recent 'wages for housework' campaign in Britain and other countries); many people in paid employment also enjoy their occupation. It is not the tax aspect, but the economic one, which is important in these cases, the point being that actual production is greater than the official figures suggest.

Sometimes, however, production can be overstated. Examples of this include people who have gone into early retirement, but who continue to be paid. This increases the national production figures on paper, but not in fact. An even more obvious case is the golden handshake. Although a company may find that it is worth paying a large sum of money in order to shed someone in this way (in other words, it derives a benefit from the payment), the fact remains that there is a recorded wage item on the books, with implied production which does not exist.

The Civil Service is not immune to these tendencies. In most developed countries today, a job in the Civil Service is as near a guarantee for one's working life as it is possible to have. Even in a period of cuts in manpower, these tend to come about by natural wastage, rather than by wholesale sacking. The British Civil Service is under constant – not always justified – attack for inefficiency and waste, and there is no doubt that it uses what we might call a disguised golden handshake, keeping people in posts when they are no longer doing the work for which they are employed. In some countries, even good civil servants are treated in this way, if they do not get on well with a minister or a civil servant of higher ranking. The person in question may be made an 'adviser' and kept on the payroll, provided that he does not take his position seriously and start giving advice. This means that in most countries for one reason or another civil servants' salaries are part of official statistics; but in economic terms their wages are not completely balanced by production.

The contribution of the British Civil Service to the national economy is officially measured by taking its total payroll, simply because we cannot think of another method. A disguised golden handshake makes production seem greater than it really is. Thus even the government contributes to distorting the picture.

There is another error, too, in the official report from the Central Statistical Office on income distribution. No blame can be attached to the CSO for this; it is virtually impossible to get at the true figures. Many people, who have to travel as part of their work, get a fixed expense allowance, which they do not have to account for afterwards. How much of it they actually spend on business is not specified, and many people get a modest but fairly regular extra income out of it. It is well known that businessmen, officials and MPs who travel abroad, or at home, may be allowed fixed expenses of first-class railway or air tickets. They may actually travel second class, and no one will ask. The same applies to hotel bills, meals and mileage allowances. The difference is extra income. This practice is neither illegal nor irregular and occurs in both the private and public sectors.

It is in those cases where expenses may have to be justified to an employer that illegal activity can come in. It is relatively easy to exaggerate the amount spent, and some people are not above putting in fictitious bills, or charging their private spending to their firms.

Payment in kind also alters income in a way which does not appear in the official figures, again without any violation of the tax laws. Payments in kind can include perks such as company cars, where the tax charged does not reflect the full benefit, or the concession made to employees allowing them to acquire goods at reduced or wholesale prices, or even free, often from associated companies. This has the effect of putting people in a higher income group than is shown in the official figures. Obtaining goods illegally occurs where people help themselves to office stationery, food from the restaurants in which they work, or 'spare parts' from their factory without permission. Employers may turn a blind eye to such activities as long as they do not get out of hand, but such actions are theft and they effectively increase income.

It is difficult to put a value on these extras. In as much as they boil down to a subjective satisfaction of human needs they cannot be measured even roughly, but even if one assesses the value of the goods used for this type of payment in kind, there remains the awkward statistical question of whether they should be taken at their cost or sales price. If they are free, the problem is even more acute.

The unofficial economy then clearly has several hidden facets, such as production, employment, unemployment, income distribution and consumption. These create a rich pattern which is both fascinating and relevant to our daily lives. As always when reality and our idea of it drift too far apart, more information is needed to establish the truth, particularly the truth as expressed in economics, sociology, politics and the law. Economists will benefit by abandoning their preoccupation with official economic figures and turning their attention to what is really happening in firms and households; sociologists of group dynamics will find much here of interest; political scientists might be able to suggest what actions politicians should take; and legal experts might realize that a regulation should not only be just but also effective.

This book discusses the unofficial economy and its causes in a neutral and descriptive way without making any moral judgement. Readers hoping for financial tips on how to raise their income or lower their expenditure or taxes will be disappointed, but everyone should understand his or her own economic position from this account of how the economy really operates.

Almost everybody comes into contact with the unofficial economy in one way or another. Some people play an active part in it by taking the initiative in various unofficial transactions, while others play a passive part by going along with them, finding that the advantages outweigh the disadvantages. There is nothing as widespread and classless in Britain, the USA or other European countries as the unofficial economy!

We should assume that the unofficial economy is large and growing, because of the clash between individual desires and norms and those of society.

Policy-makers need a better insight into the whole phenomenon, so that they can take steps towards reconciling official with unofficial economic patterns; too much official effort in the past has gone into, for example, the ludicrous operations of VAT officers, like counting the grains of rice in a portion in a restaurant to try to calculate the accuracy of invoices, photographing people in shops, and raiding stockbrokers' offices, which involved the Inland Revenue in relatively trivial court cases. Spectacular though these actions may appear, it is arguable whether they are consistent with our current legal concepts – a question that will be turned to later in the book.

2 A simple model of the economy

In scientific research, one frequently comes across phenomena which appear too vast or too complex to be understood completely and immediately. To overcome this, students begin by concentrating on a simplified picture of reality, a *model*. A matrix is one type of model; other possible forms are a drawing, or a scientific experiment, or a set of equations, or even an abstract picture in one's mind. Models are an intellectual bypass which enable us to detect basic relationships, and from them go on to elaborate new hypotheses. Once the characteristics of a phenomenon have been established on this simple level, we can get nearer to reality by eliminating some of the simple issues. This leads to the building of a new model, more complex than the former, which allows for more refined conclusions. Each time the cycle is repeated, the results will be better, more realistic and, in the case of practical matters, more operational.

Even after constant repetition, however, the way in which reality is represented in a model remains a more or less sketchy outline, especially when dealing with social problems. Any process that is wholly or partly determined by human behaviour is bound to be more complicated than the most elaborate model, which can never allow for irrational actions. Nevertheless, the gradual approach described above is so far the most efficient method found for coping with problems whose size or complexity prevents them from being directly and fully accessible to the human mind.

In economics the use of models to reach broad conclusions is common. One of the best known examples is in representing the overall economy of a country as a set of flows. In this system, commodities move from producers to consumers. As they are paid for, money flows in the opposite direction. The core of a simple economic model consists therefore of a flow of goods moving from producers to consumers, and a consequent flow of money in the opposite direction (see figure 1, page 19).

Even at first glance, this picture is a very poor representation of reality. It does not reflect, for instance, commodities which go abroad, or are transmitted from one producer to another, rather than to a consumer. Furthermore, it does not show how money is paid into a savings bank or to the tax man. An acceptable image of real life obviously demands a complete network of flows. Before attempting to design such a network, however, we have some observations to make which are of a more general nature.

In the first place, a few words about the aim of this book. For professional economists, model building is rewarding anyhow, since it helps them to satisfy their scientific curiosity. Non-economists, on the other hand, would probably find such exercises too academic and of little incentive towards understanding. In any case, our motive in introducing this method is quite different. We prefer the flow model, because it is such an excellent instrument for the *measurement* of the economic process. A flow has two characteristics – a direction and a size. If we are able to establish the latter, we can get not only a picture of the structure of the country's economy, but also of the quantities involved. It goes without saying that such information is of the utmost importance in managing a country.

We shall shortly deal with the techniques of measurement, but we must emphasize right away that no precise measurement can be expected. We will have to make do with approximations, blurred pictures. In addition, the measurement will turn out to be not only imprecise, but also incomplete, for certain flows are partly or entirely impossible to observe – these are the flows of the unofficial economy. Arithmetically speaking, the official and underground economies add up to reality.

Finally, a few remarks on terminology. So far, we have written of producers making goods. Many producers, however, do not produce goods in the usual sense of the word – they perform services instead. This happens when one describes the activities of, say, lawyers, fortune tellers, hotels, cobblers, schools, beauty parlours, taxi drivers, dancers and singers, or public swimming pools. For the sake of completeness, therefore, we ought to refer to 'goods and services'. To avoid this lengthy phrase, we will use the word 'goods' to include both categories, a convention not uncommon among economists. In using the word 'goods', therefore, we will be referring to everything actually produced, both material commodities and services – unless the text clearly indicates a contrary definition.

In fact, we will avoid using the words 'producer' and 'consumer' altogether in this chapter, because they suggest that we are referring to particular individuals. In our network of flows, attention is focused on centres of activity of economic relevance which are best designated as 'production unit' and 'consumption unit' (or, less precisely, 'family unit').

Circular flow diagrams

We begin by representing the national economy in the simplest possible way. All production units are gathered together in a single entity, the production sector, P. Similarly, all family units are compressed into the consumptions sector, C. Goods move from P to C, and money streams in return from C to P.

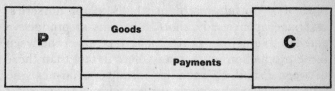

Obviously, this process will soon stop. The goods are consumed in C, so we need not bother about their destination, but the question is, where does the money come from and what happens to it in the end? The answer to these questions is that a second flow of money exists, going from P to C, brought about by the wages firms pay to their employees. This means that the money flow is really circular in shape.

To complete the diagram, we now add a fourth flow, which represents labour on its way from C to P. The model now looks like this:

```
┌──────┐ ┌─ Goods ──────────────┐ ┌──────┐
│      │ │    ── Payments ──     │ │      │
│  P   │ │  ── Wages ──          │ │  C   │
│      │ │      ── Work ──       │ │      │
└──────┘ └──────────────────────┘ └──────┘
```

Incidentally, labour is only one of several elements which C provides P with against payment. There are family units which put other *production factors* as well at P's disposal; these arise in the form of interest, rent or profit. However, it is not necessary to over-complicate the diagram by including all these separate flows.

It is true, too, that the most drastic simplification we have introduced into the model is in the aggregating of the whole of production. The unassuming box P stands for a vast range of activities – factories, shops, hospitals, knife sharpening, nuclear power stations, tax consultants, dance halls, plant nurseries, marriage agencies: in short, all forms of productive activity. Numerous transactions take place between these production units, many more in fact than those between P and C. Take, for instance, a farmer who sells his heifer to a cattle dealer, who in turn sells it to a butcher who transports it to the slaughterhouse. The heifer's skin goes to the tanner who sells the leather to a shoe factory. The shoes end up, via a retail shop, eventually at sector C. The heifer's meat follows other channels, but will ultimately reach the consumption area as well. Some by-products will be processed by the chemical industry, for medical and other uses; others will be sold to the farmer to help him raise heifers in a more efficient way. There seems no end to the possible ramifications of the network.

It is impossible to show all these transactions between individual units in one simple diagram, and the resulting maze would be too complicated to be of any use. What can be done, however (and actually *is* done), is to divide sector P into a number of technically related groups (classes of industry), and each of these again into sub-groups (industries). Even this simplification of reality is still too much for a handy diagram, and inter-relations are usually shown in a kind of accounting system.

Let us now go back to the primary structure of the

network, which is suitable for graphic representation. In order to make our diagram more realistic, we now introduce a third sector (the first two being P and C) for the government, G. This new sector is usually also subdivided, the components being central or national government, local authorities, and the social security system.

The question immediately arises of whether the introduction of this new sector is justified. After all, government appears to be just another conglomerate of production units which provide certain services (such as street lighting, education, police protection, and roads) for which they are paid by the users in some form or another. It is therefore arguable that government should be regarded as a part of sector P, rather than as an independent sector in its own right. Such a conclusion, however, neglects several essential aspects. To begin with, the government provides certain services which no private firm could perform, at least not in the same quality, such as legislation, jurisdiction, and national defence. Services of this kind constitute the core of governmental activity; hence they can be called 'public' or 'collective' goods. Secondly, the government offers certain services the use of which is compulsory for all, or certain, categories of inhabitants. Examples are primary and secondary education, social security, and land registration. Thirdly, the way we pay for most of the government's services differs fundamentally from all other transactions. This aspect will be dealt with extensively in a later chapter. For the time being, it is enough to say that we all pay taxes and, in so doing, feed the government's coffers with contributions which are at best only marginally related to the use any one individual makes of the public services. People who never leave their homes in the evening are nevertheless obliged to pay their share of the cost of street lighting. People who never travel abroad are not allowed tax concessions, although they do not benefit from the consulates the government maintains in foreign countries. Families who send their children to private schools nonetheless contribute to the state system of education through their rates and taxes. Even if a citizen feels opposed to a given action of government, such as the distribution of financial support for the arts, or membership of NATO, he cannot stop a fraction of his money being spent for such purposes. A recent case where a woman attempted to transfer that part of her tax payment which went on defence to peaceful purposes failed in her attempt under the tax laws, which do not allow individuals to choose where the tax they pay goes.

The specific nature of the governmental sector is perhaps most clearly brought to light by an analysis of an altogether different part of its activities. A proportion of tax revenue is not used to cover the costs of services provided, but is transferred in cash, without any compensation, to firms and households, in the form, for example, of industrial allowances or social security payments. These payments are, of course, not related at all to the tax paid by the beneficiaries. (If they were, the operation would be pointless.) The aim is rather to *re*distribute the national income and national wealth. It is a matter of national solidarity imposed by law.

It is true, nevertheless, that in certain other aspects government behaves much like private enterprise. It can only perform its duties when – like any entrepreneur – it employs labour, owns buildings, buys equipment, borrows money and ... pays for all these things. But there are differences. The legal status of a civil servant (not to speak of a conscript) is not absolutely identical to that of a private employer, but these differences are of a formal nature, and do not in themselves justify the creation of a separate sector *G* in the model. The diagram has now been extended:

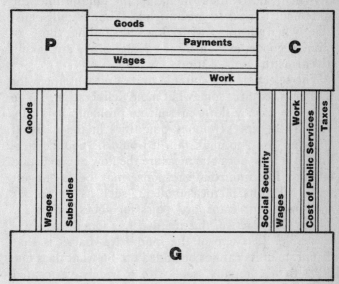

A full representation of a country's economy, however, requires a fourth element, an overseas sector, *O*. Money, goods, and production factors cross national borders in both directions. This is what happens in the cases of imports and exports, tourism, foreign labour in domestic industry, overseas investment, and financial dealings with international organizations. There are many flows between this sector *O* and the sectors *P, C* and *G*.

Measuring the flows

When a technician says that five gallons of liquid pass through a certain pipe, the immediate response will be: five gallons a second, a minute or an hour? He has given the unit of measurement (gallon) and the quantity (five), but without including the unit of time, the statement is next to meaningless. Time is indispensable when dealing with flows, including those of money, goods, etc. In these examples, we are taking a year as the unit of time.

The selection of a suitable unit of measurement for the flows requires somewhat more deliberation. To be sure, the money flows present no problem: it is only natural to express money quantities in the national currency unit; so in Britain it would be pounds sterling. But how does one measure the flow of goods and labour? The immediate response may be to suggest technical units of measurement, such as tonnes for coal, miles for transport, pairs for shoes, hours for labour. In practice, this method was found to be unworkable. Just one of the many drawbacks is that disparate units cannot be added up. So what does one do with a company, say, with a widely variegated production range, say 12,000 kinds of hardware? Even a one-product organization, such as a cigar factory, would cause problems since there are many varieties of cigars. Moreover, each separate cigar factory probably produces its own types and brands, so that one is still at a loss as to how to aggregate the whole cigar industry.

In short, difficulties abound where material goods are concerned. And the situation is even worse in the area of services. There is no common-sense unit of measurement for transportation at large, for the vast range of medical services, for banks, for all the experts we pay for information or advice. The flows of labour do not offer any more relief. Initially, perhaps, the hour might seem to be an appropriate yardstick, but total human labour is made up of such widely diverging activities that the simple addition of all the time-units worked would scarcely have any meaning.

The long and short of it is that technical units of measurement will not do. A comprehensive description of the economic process requires a dimension which is common to all flows of goods – and preferably to other flows as well. This would lead to a measurement applicable to every sort of flow. Since the common measure is unlikely to be found by concentrating on the physical quantities of goods and labour, let us investigate another measure, that of value.

Value happens to be one of those basic concepts of economics on which scholars have been brooding endlessly, and which has been defined in many different ways. Fortunately, in this context, we need not concern ourselves with such niceties. The type of value we have in mind is a simple arithmetic notion, that of physical quantity multiplied by price; in other words, an amount that can be readily found on any invoice, bill, payslip, cash register tape, etc. Value in this sense is always expressed in money. There is, therefore, a common unit of measurement for all flows of goods and labour. It is the unit of currency, and for Britain this means the pound sterling. In this way we arrive at the same yardstick as that already selected for the money flows.

The Central Statistical Office builds up its picture of the country's economy by gathering together a vast number of figures provided by government agencies, industry, trade unions, the Inland Revenue, the customs and excise authorities, and various other bodies. From these figures it reaches its conclusions about the level of gross national product, gross domestic product, retail sales, employment and unemployment, inflation and a number of other figures which together provide a comprehensive picture of the official economy. That these figures do not produce a mirror image of what exactly happens in real life can be illustrated by looking at the official figures for employment, to begin with; the definition of those 'economically active' excludes many people who are actually working. Employment and unemployment statistics describe people aged fifteen and over who are registered as employed or unemployed. So the figures immediately exclude housewives working in their own home, or in someone else's home if they do not declare the income from the work. Students working during the vacation do not come into the figures, nor do the young who do small jobs like newspaper delivery, or of course the vast army doing jobs for a cash return, which they do not declare to the Inland Revenue. This means that the figures for those in work are almost invariably understated. No blame can be attributed to the CSO for these shortcomings: the data are simply not available.

At the same time, unemployment figures, too, can be understated. Those married women, for example, who are still allowed not to pay full national insurance contributions and choose not to, very often do not appear in unemployment figures. They simply do not bother to register as unemployed, because they are not eligible for unemployment benefits.

Similarly, the statistics published for gross domestic product do not actually reflect reality. Officially, GDP is the value of goods and services produced by residents of the United Kingdom, including taxes on expenditure on both home and imported goods and services less subsidies. Clearly any production as a result of 'moonlighting' is not included in this. Then, GDP includes only those incomes of residents which arise directly from the current production of goods and services and this in turn excludes any income from any moonlighting. Any income, like social security payments, which is paid without any service (or product) being received in return is also excluded. Most official statistics are therefore subject to some distortion in several directions and the nearer we can come to measuring the level of them, the closer we will be to assessing the true size of the unofficial economy and to dealing with it.

After this important step, we begin to see the light. Using the currency unit as the measuring unit means that different kinds of goods and different kinds of labour within a given firm can be totalled. Next, the figures of all individual firms of a given industry can be aggregated, and so on. Eventually, the whole turnover of a country can be expressed in one single amount, the gross domestic product. Another advantage of this method is, of course, that money movements and other flows are measured by the same unit. This implies that any two paired flows (say, labour and wages, or goods and payments) are of equal size. It is therefore enough to measure one of them.

This method also has certain drawbacks. For instance, one is at a loss in comparing the figures concerning two different years, if (as nowadays is always the case) the prices have changed in the meantime. This aspect does not affect the subject of this book, however, and we shall therefore not elaborate on it.

A more important question is how the measurement

is carried out in practice. Apart from an overall report on the country's economy during a whole year, the government also publishes partial results over shorter periods. Monthly and quarterly data on unemployment, cost of living, the level of production, retail sales, foreign trade, etc. can be found in the newspapers. This intermediary information, too, depicts the official economy; that is, the officially observed part of reality.

Where is the borderline?

So far, we have defined the unofficial economy as the gap between reality and official economy. The latter has been described in some detail, but much less has been said about the notion of 'reality'. This vagueness has, of course, certain repercussions in assessing the size of the unofficial economy. We shall therefore endeavour to outline the various concepts with greater precision.

The fundamental concept is that official economy, unofficial economy, and reality correspond to the same pattern, namely they each produce an image of a network of flows of money, goods, and production factors. It is worth mentioning that stocks of money, goods, or labour may amass between various flows, and that these stocks also belong to the system. In short, reality, the official economy, and the unofficial economy are identical in structure. But the range of elements from which the structure is built, that is, the above flows and stocks, is different in all three.

We have already dealt with the sizes relevant to the official economy. They are the published results of the activities of the Central Statistical Office and similar agencies. The official economy can therefore be defined as the officially registered part of reality. It seems to be the time to have a look at reality itself.

By 'reality' we mean here nothing profound, philosophical, or metaphysical. All we are thinking of is the real movement of economic flows and stocks, irrespective of their being measured or not. We could have chosen another term, such as 'integral economy' or 'total economy'. The only importance is to define what does and what does not belong to reality. This is entirely a matter of convention. We have already noticed that the notion of 'goods' is often taken by economists in the broad sense to include services as well as material products. However, this by no means implies that every human effort or activity should be absorbed into this notion. When a woman washes her hair, she is no doubt performing a useful act, but there would be no point in including such a socially irrelevant event in the economic process. It is much more practical to define 'reality' in a way that leaves such activities out.

Conversely, when a hairdresser washes a customer's hair, we do want to include that work in the economic process, so that it will eventually become part of either the official or the unofficial economy (according to whether or not it has been registered in the official statistics).

Examples of actions which may or may not have an economic impact and which are aimed to directly satisfy the needs of the performer, or of a member of his family, are common throughout society. Economics, it is true, is the science that deals with human needs and resources in a very wide sense; we will limit ourselves for the purpose of this book to those needs which are satisfied by means of transactions. This concept excludes all activities of the family within the household – housework, all DIY jobs, vegetable gardening for consumption, in short, any 'self-providing' activity. To set the concept in terms of the model: it consists of flows *between* units (production or consumption units), but never *within* a unit.

It is also advisable to neglect certain parts of the flows between consumption units. Transfers like personal gifts or friendly help are best ignored, not so much because they do not answer the criterion, but rather because such shifts in purchasing power are of no relevance to policy-making. This is about the point where conceptual difficulties begin to crop up. What about gifts of unusually great value, say, a house as a wedding present for a daughter or son? Ought we to ignore the barter of friendly services in the style of 'young Michael will babysit tonight, if your daughter will wash our car tomorrow'? Similar problems may arise when a non-professional photographer pleases his acquaintances with a few snapshots. As long as he is reimbursed for his costs, the situation is clear, but hobbies often grow into a source of additional earnings, and one cannot always be sure about the exact demarcation. Even activities within the household can be an area of doubt, especially when one does jobs at home which are an everyday part of one's work: a good example is a self-employed builder who builds his own house, but the list is endless. There are international conventions on these questions, but new borderline cases constantly arise. This whole demarcation issue is not a central problem in the analysis of the official economy, but it does sometimes raise peripheral questions of some importance.

One curious detail is perhaps still worth mentioning. As a consequence of the chosen criterion, that is, a transaction has taken place, the size of an economic flow may be altered by the sole fact that the performance of a given activity is transferred to another person. This can happen in the case of hairwashing, as we have seen. The same phenomenon also occurs when an invalid relative who has been taken care of at home moves into a hospital or residential home, or when one changes from taking the bus, tube, or car to walking to work in the morning. Similarly, the hiring of a butler, the use of a laundry, eating out rather than at home, or changing from following a paying language course to self-study, all have an impact on the size of economic activity. It goes without saying that in each of these examples, the movement can be in the opposite direction. The most disconcerting conclusion is perhaps that economic figures may be modified as a result of a purely formal change in the state of affairs, without any new activity arising. The classical example of this is the widower's housekeeper who marries her employer, and subsequently becomes a housewife. Although she continues performing exactly the same chores, her work is no longer included in the national statistics, because she is no longer a wage earner.

It will be clear from the above exposition that our 'reality' largely covers the system that economists used to call 'the economic circuit'. Still, there are a few divergences. In the view of the traditional economist, income only came about when consumption units provided production units with production factors, and received in exchange wage, rent or profit. Private property only arose when such a consumption unit did not fully spend its income. There was a time when this model provided a satisfactory picture of society. The world keeps changing, however, and economics, as much as any other science, has to adapt its conceptual tools continually. The first old age pensions paid to retired employees – voluntarily, and not based on any insurance system – were seen as gifts provided by generous employers from their own pockets. They were thought to manifest a noble character trait, but were of no interest to the economist. Only much later were these payments recognized as postponed wages which deserved a flow of their own in the diagram. Today, all transfers of income by the government are taken to be part of the system, even if they are not based on an insurance plan, such as social security allowances.

The time has now come to widen the concepts of economics once again. The link between income and productive effort tends to become increasingly looser, and a growing number of economists are in favour of severing the two completely. Would it therefore not be more realistic to widen the income concept as to comprise any acquisition of purchasing power, whatever the source? If we accept this, income (and property) would not only be the result of one's work or investments, of one's pension or state allowance, or of saving, but also of cashing a forged cheque, or of winning a bet. This seems contradictory to what we just proposed, i.e. the exclusion of small gifts and services between friends. This is indeed so, but the latter suggestion is based not on a matter of principle, but on its feasibility.

It is not necessary to stress that our proposals are based on a modernization of statistical categories, not on a reform of the legal system. Theft should not be penalized less than it is, just because stolen property is allocated a place in the model.

If these new varieties of income and property are

'recognized', establishing their size presents a problem. But measurement is beset with difficulties in any case, witness the unofficial economy. We shall deal with the latter in some detail in the next section.

The origins of the unofficial economy

We have broadly outlined how the economic process functions in our type of society, and how the government establishes the quantities involved. We have then pointed out that the results of this measurement reflect only a part of reality, and that the remainder, the unofficial economy, deserves more attention than it is given at present. In a later chapter, we shall examine the significance of the unofficial economy from a policy viewpoint. For the time being, we are merely describing the phenomenon and need to deal with such questions as, Why is the official measurement so incomplete? What kind of leakages prevent the observation of certain flows in their full size? Are we confronted with errors, or technical imperfections, or sabotage, or lack of goodwill? Or are these gaps inherent to the society in which we live?

Since the unofficial economy has been defined as the not-officially-registered part of the economic reality, we will begin by looking for those economic activities whose registration is intentionally omitted by the persons involved in the first place. Such cases are not difficult to detect. People whose professional activities are in conflict with the law will try to leave as few traces of their business as possible, both on paper and otherwise. This holds primarily for income obtained from outright criminal sources, like theft, fraud, or counterfeiting. Activities like poaching, pickpocketing, and smuggling may legally speaking be of a lesser calibre, but they fall equally under this category.

The same holds true for professions where the activity is not illegal in itself, but carried out without the required licence, as in the case of secret gambling saloons. However, all these legal distinctions are of little weight in our argument. The essence is that certain members of our society draw their incomes illegally and the risk of detection and punishment induces them to omit recording their dealings. One cannot expect a burglar to keep neat accounts, so that he can complete annual returns of his turnover.

Akin to the preceding category are certain other professions where keeping records is also rare, but where fear of sanctions is not the motive. These are activities which are legally forbidden but in practice never prosecuted since the authorities feel that the law is no longer in accordance with today's ethics. Other gaps in official figures arise in those cases where perpetrators *are* prosecuted, but systematically never found guilty, or even such where sanctions are imposed but never carried into effect. Again, all these procedural niceties are not at the heart of our subject-matter. What really is at issue is the fact that among the population there are procurers, soft-drug pushers, quack doctors, and the like, who all think their legally marginal position to be a good reason for not keeping any record of their incomes.

In short, all those whose profession involves the breaking of a law, even if they are not prosecuted, contribute to the unofficial economy. We shall now leave this colourful assembly, but we must remain for a moment in the sphere of illegality. As it is, many offences are committed in the framework of an otherwise respectable profession. Accounts are kept, but unlawful acts are omitted from them. Again, the legal characteristics are irrelevant for our purposes. The sins of a building contractor who constructs a conservatory without having a building permit, a businessman who organizes a fraudulent bankruptcy, or a shopkeeper who doctors his scales, may, legally (and also morally) speaking, belong to different classes, but in one aspect they come to the same: it is wise to have no illusions about correctly defining them as lawbreakers.

All these remarks concern people who have a business or are self-employed in a profession. On the whole, they keep their own accounts. The situation is different for wage-earners as their income is normally recorded as well by their employers, but broadly speaking at least they are capable of similar activities: illegal acts are not registered, and hence will not be reflected in the official statistics. A manual worker who takes a tool home, a secretary the office stationery, a travelling salesman who submits false costs claims and a squatter who pays no rent all enjoy a fragment of income the official figures do not tell us anything about.

So far we have dealt with cases where registration was omitted because the activity was somehow unlawful. On the other hand, perfectly 'clean' acts are also quite frequently omitted from the books, or entered in a distorted way. The motives for this behaviour are generally to procure financial advantages. Everyone has heard of firms that manage to curtail their profits or turnover in their accounts, or shift them to other countries. Employees, although they keep no books of their income, take the same attitude. They conceal the proceeds of evening jobs, or the rent from letting part of their property; they manipulate inheritances, capital transfers and insurances. Tax avoidance has many ramifications, which we shall tackle in a separate chapter.

All these deliberate decisions not to register turnover, income, gifts in kind, etc. have one feature in common – they are the roots of 'black' money, money the owners officially do not own. Whatever the origin of these possessions, the owners suffer from the same predicament: they have to organize their expenditure in such a way that the authorities get no hint of the existence of their non-registered riches. The simplest way to this end is a moderate expansion of current consumption. A new home, nicer food, better furniture, a bigger car or longer holiday trips: all these and similar purchases help the money lose its 'blackness' from the moment it enters the till of the supermarket store or hotel. Ostentatious spending, say, on a yacht or an extremely expensive car is, on the other hand, bound to attract the attention of the police or the tax man. So there are constraints.

If really big amounts are at stake, it is obviously advisable to keep the money for some time, and then spend it piecemeal. People who keep money tend to invest it in a variety of ways, including the stock market. In these cases the 'black' money turns 'white' but will eventually re-acquire its blackness. If the owner is to conceal his assets the interest earned will not be declared and this, too, will go unaccounted for. As a result, there will eventually be even more 'black' money than before.

It is often said that 'black' investors during their apprenticeship often try their luck with investments, about which they are largely ignorant. They are, therefore, frequently easy game for a new class of intermediaries who 'help' them with the most fantastic pieces of advice and commercial offers. Information on the resulting dealings is difficult to get, but it seems safe to assume that many of the stories circulating about stamp collections, precious stones, villas in Spain, German bordello shares, plots of land in America and other exotics (all purchased at prices far above the current value) are indeed true. Of course, 'white' savings can be tricked into such adventures as well, but their owners at least have some possibility of regaining their money through legal action. 'Black' investors naturally shun such steps because they fear that police investigation will reveal the origin of the money. If rumours are to be believed, these dealings go beyond simple swindling into the realms of blackmail.

It is best that we refrain from evaluating the social aspects of this phenomenon, which does not bear directly on the subject of this book. But it is worth noting that the money does not necessarily and fully leave the unofficial economy by such transactions. On the contrary, it can get deeper into the core of it. One could say that a part is transferred from the commercially 'black' sphere to the criminally 'black' sphere: the whereabouts of a certain fraction of the circulating money is unknown.

We return once more to the people who own 'black' money, and have to decide how to spend it. In fact, immediate consumption and investment are not the only options. Owners of small firms often prefer to recycle the money withdrawn for fiscal reasons from their business. They put it back into the same business where it can be productive. This can be done quite openly, pretending that the 'new' money stems from one's private fortune. It is nevertheless a risky procedure since the Inland Revenue might at any time ask just where these private riches have originated. Of course, one could claim that it comes from gambling, betting, or a lottery* but that does not sound very credible to the tax man. There are far more subtle techniques for laundering 'black' money. Fake transactions in the accounts would do the job.

Many small business people go about the problem in other ways. They leave the 'black' money where it is, and use it for the payment of 'black' wages and 'black' raw materials. 'Black' transactions may gather together, and eventually grow into complete 'black' circuits. In the segments of the national economy where these practices have currency, the individual businessman has no choice. If he cannot buy material or hire staff without paying a 'black' premium, he will have to join the game, or his business will not flourish.

The above explanations might create the impression that the underground economy springs exclusively from crime, clandestinity, fraud, and other unlawful acts. Such a picture would be grossly incomplete. The so-called black economy is doubtlessly an important component of the unofficial economy; one may even call it the core, but still it is only a part.

To begin with the most popular subject, taxation: not all tax avoidance is of a fraudulent nature. In fact, our fiscal laws are studded with provisions on allowances, exemptions, permissible profit shifts, and many more. Taxpayers are also left some discretion in the design of tax-saving schemes. In short, the range of lawful possibilities is so wide and variegated that many books are published on the subject, and an

* In some countries, the winner of a lottery prize can sell his lucky ticket at a ten-per-cent premium. The purchaser is, of course, an owner of 'black' money.

army of advisers busy themselves daily with the implementation of such schemes. But however legal these means are, they often lead to a divergence between the economic reality and its registration, and therefore have a bearing on the unofficial economy.

The unofficial economy in the sense in which we use the word is not only a matter of income, profit, turnover, and similar fiscal quantities. There are other economic categories whose size is measured in a dubious way. One example is absence from work for health reasons. The tendency of lost working days to increase is quite plausible in itself. More diseases are determined, nowadays, and modern treatments may require more time. Moreover, there is often change in the ideas about how serious a complaint should be to justify absence from work: the threshold is dropping constantly. All these explanations, of course, provide no indication on the residue, the malingerers. Nobody knows their number but all experts agree that the official figures do not reflect reality. Unemployment is another example. People still manage to get unemployment pay while they are actually working, because the authorities do not, in fact cannot, check on everyone who may be moonlighting. These examples are not the only ones either. There are more official statistics concerning the application of social security laws which, according to experts, are a far cry from real life.

Quite different matters are the official indices for the cost of living. These indices are based on the retail price levels. But do households pay these prices in fact on the average? There is a growing tendency to look for cheaper opportunities, especially – though not exclusively – in respect of the larger items of household equipment. People are bargaining in shops far more often these days. They try to buy directly from wholesalers, or get access to the retailers' selling points, or shop abroad. The official measurement lags behind these developments.

Conclusion

The development of new concepts is – at least in a science like economics – by no means a straightforward process. The researcher advances, hesitating and groping in order to catch the correct phrasing for his theories. When he ultimately puts his brainchild to paper, he knows full well that he is still far from the stage of achievement. We, too, had to follow this route when we developed the notion of the unofficial economy.

The reader will certainly have noticed traces of a zigzagging approach in this chapter, especially where we have tried to set the limits and the contents of the new theory precisely. We believe, however, that it was right to come out into the open right at the start. In fact, the problem we meet is not primarily a matter of designing or defining a theory, but rather one of policy implementation techniques. During the debates which undoubtedly will follow, experts from various areas will, we hope, point out examples of imperfect measurement of the economic process in their fields. Such material will help to better define the limits of the phenomenon in question. In the course of this process the most operational definition will automatically emerge.

After all, the argument is about an utterly practical problem. Our contention is that the official figures now published as a quantitative description, of the economic process diverge in various aspects so drastically from real events that they are a risky basis for policy decisions. If the government wants to rectify the situation, it will somehow have to secure the restraint of the unofficial economy, or reform the measuring methods so that they yield a more reliable copy of economy reality. Whether it wants this or not is a matter of policy. The mix of the two remedies again is a policy option.

Our criticism is aimed not only at the results of the official gauging of the flows which constitute the classical image of the economic circuit, but also the governmental indices and indications for, say, unemployment and the cost of living. To resume, any subject of official statistics taken into consideration, for designing or implementing policies, may be a constituent of the unofficial economy.

The criterion chosen for our criticism of the present outcome of measurement, that is, the relevance to policy decisions, requires concentration on the *measurable* part of reality. Although we are deeply convinced that economics should in the last resort deal with psychological variables, in this chapter we have had to stick to elements with a monetary value, or at least a numeric dimension. In practice, the choice is further limited to those elements for which feasible measurement methods exist. To be sure, measurement should be understood in a larger sense, that is including acceptable estimation techniques. Still, some of the examples may reveal that our views on this measurability are a bit too optimistic.

To demonstrate the argument, we shall elaborate on the extension of the idea of *income* we advocate. Generations of economists have been brought up with the idea that the remuneration for the availability of a production factor is the only conceivable source of income. However, the rise of new social or economic structures forced them gradually to extend this notion. As we have already pointed out, employees' pensions, originally looked at as a product of charity, have eventually been considered as postponed wages. Today, they are a clear part of total income, albeit at a secondary indirect level. At a later stage, that part of the government's function which relates to the redistribution of national income – whether through social security or directly, in the form of allowances to individuals and subsidies on certain products – results in transfers which have no productive counterpart equally under our idea of income.

We are going one step further. For the purposes of the unofficial economy study, we shall take income to include not only transfers effectuated by the government or the insurance mechanism, but also any transmission of purchasing power through other, non-official channels. We have shown that these channels are partly situated in legally or morally forbidden fields, but that is no reason to exclude their effects from economic reality, nor to neglect the measurement of these effects. The tax authorities, incidentally – traditionally the most consequent realists in the Civil Service – also ignore legal and moral criteria as regards the origins of their clients' incomes.

Such extensions of this theory of income require a redefinition of the boundaries. We are including all four categories; that is, productive income, postponed income, officially transferred income, and factually transmitted income. The minimum requirement is a shift of money or goods between two units of production, or consumption. Any further extension would certainly ignore the need of measurability.

The implication is that we have not dealt in this

chapter with 'psychological income', however useful this concept may be in other fields of economic research. We have already been led to exclude all 'self-providing' activities on the same grounds. We should, however, note that there are also economists who rather accentuate this form of production.* They expect that our society will evolve into a 'self-service economy' in which the self-providing activity (called 'the informal sector') will have a central position, and where any production outside the consumption sector will only serve to provide each household with the equipment. We do not dismiss such future views by any means, but for the present they are of no help in the study of today's unofficial economy.

The exclusion of self-providing activities from the official economic situations – the consequence of an international convention agreed upon decades ago – has recently also been criticized from a quite different angle. As the work in consumption units (say, households) is mainly performed by women, the ignoring of this kind of labour in official statistics could be interpreted as a form of discrimination. We should like to stress that this impression rests on a misunderstanding. Self-providing is left out, because this activity takes place outside the market circuit, and consequently no measurement in the usual sense of the word is possible. Should housewife wages, as suggested by groups in several countries, ever come about, the definition of income would, of course, have to be adapted to the new situation.

---

* See Jonathan Gershuny *After Industrial Society? The Emerging Self-Service Economy*, London 1978.

3 Citizen v. government: a never-ending struggle

Since time began, people have joined together to create facilities which they cannot afford as individuals. Adventurers went on voyages of discovery in mutually owned and equipped ships; believers in God founded congregations in order to build a church; nature lovers, eager to save threatened kinds of animals, have started conservation groups and workers have formed unions to protect their jobs. The participants may make the desired facilities through their own work, but they may also leave expert jobs to craftsmen, contributing to the common aim by paying a share in the cost.

There is more than one method for apportioning the cost out among the members of a group. One possible way is to charge an entrance fee when entering a church so that financial contributions are proportional to the frequency of use; on the other hand, money may be raised by voluntary collections and fund-raising activities. The simplest way to raise the funds needed is by all members paying an equal sum. Such an arrangement can be modified and adapted through a system of lower contributions through allowances for those who have a low income, support a larger family, or have a low financial capacity for some other reason.

Another possible technique of apportionment is through insurance. This is simply a form of financial cooperation to cover the losses that one of the members might incur as a consequence of a future event which may or may not happen. Each individual pays a small amount only, because only a few will need the funds. Illness or the death of a breadwinner are typical examples of need. To protect themselves against uncertainties of this kind, the participants create a fund to which they each contribute regularly. If a mishap occurs for one of the members, he or she will be allowed an indemnification from the fund.

Modern states are organized in patterns which resemble these forms of cooperation in many respects. There is one important difference, however: affiliation to the group is not voluntary. Any person (as well as any object) within a state's territory automatically comes under its authority. As a consequence, the managing body of the state, that is, the government, can require contributions from the inhabitants to meet the cost of common facilities. It can even forcibly collect such contributions. The compulsory character of this financial solidarity by no means applies to certain types of state only. In a democracy, where any claim by the government has to be previously approved by the elected representatives of the people, the situation is the same as in a totalitarian state – in fact, no other solution is conceivable. Democratic countries have specific procedures for making laws, but once a particular law is in force, the individual citizen no longer has freedom in the area covered by it. When this comes to financial contributions required by the government from its citizens, each individual is obliged to pay his share, even if he does not agree with the techniques of apportionment, or if he believes that the facilities his money have helped to acquire are superfluous or even harmful.

The last part of the preceding statement is a bit too sweeping. Certain contributions are levied, like the church entrance fees we have described. This means that people only pay if they make use of the facility. This happens when one travels by train or consumes electric power. Anyone not requiring these services does not have to use them, and need not contribute to their cost – at least not directly. At first sight, it appears then that the government is behaving like an ordinary business, submitting to the rules of the market game. This, however, is an illusion.

To begin with, the types of goods and services provided by the government are usually not available elsewhere. They include water from the mains, sewage, the issue of passports, postal services, many types of education, and the police. They constitute vital necessities to many people, so that an individual's freedom to take or leave them is merely academic. Secondly, a government can manipulate the prices it charges in ways an ordinary businessman could not afford, at least for any length of time. Indeed, it can offer facilities at a non-profit-making price, or even at a loss. Sometimes, the price is a formality, a mere symbolic compensation which bears no relationship whatsoever to the cost of production. Examples include subsidized travel fares, university fees and further education. The amounts in question clearly are nil prices in the economic sense; we will refer to them as *pseudo-prices*.

Then there are payments to the government which do not even resemble prices, but are like fixed membership fees. Every citizen is subject to them, irrespective of the use he or she is making of the public facilities. For instance, everyone has to hand over a part of his income to the government without being entitled to a specific *quid pro quo*. It is impossible to say where the contributions of a given individual go;

the money is simply added to the 'general fund'. This is the pool from which the government pays the cost of its operations, including the losses we have just referred to. These government levies without specific benefits are known to everyone – they are called *taxes*.

A third type of financial contribution is collected on the insurance principle. It has something in common with pseudo-prices and taxes. On one hand, it resembles taxes because affiliation is compulsory – as a rule at least. But the proceeds are not amalgamated with the general fund; they are held separately for specific payments. In this respect, they are closer to pseudo-prices. Their name is *premiums*, and they are most clearly and largely represented by national insurance contributions.

The above outline is not extensive enough to cover the precise classification of all government revenue, but we do not need that for the purposes of this book. Anyway, there are differences of opinion about it and ideas are changing about how it should be categorized. In certain countries, for instance, there is a tendency to look at social security payments as a sub-species of taxes; in others, conversely, there are plans to intensify the relation between payment and performance in this area.

As far as the average citizen is concerned, however, there is no clear distinction between taxes and social security payments. In view of the existing collection techniques, this attitude is quite understandable. National insurance is deducted by the employer from wages, so that it is small wonder that people see it as an extension of income tax. All our remarks about taxes in this chapter will, therefore, generally speaking, apply equally to social security payments.

So far we have presented all public levies as a means

of dividing the cost of the government's services among its citizens. Historically speaking, this may indeed be so, but in modern times governments have widened the purpose of their activities. No tax is really neutral in its effect – it will always bring changes in the social tissue. Originally, these shifts were regarded as unavoidable side-effects, but today the authorities use pseudo-prices, taxes, and social security payments as policy instruments, precisely because of these effects. For instance, taxation can be used to control consumption as in the case when products like tobacco or alcohol, which can be damaging to health, are made more expensive by heavy taxation than they need be, to deter people from using them. Other levies, say high import duties to protect domestic industry, can be used for their economic effects. The more general objectives of economic policy, such as control of business cycles, can also be achieved by fiscal measures: to quote just one example – tax allowances designed to encourage capital investment in industry which in turn helps to create employment.

The most comprehensive function of public finance today is to smooth out differences in wealth between people. We shall soon see this in more detail when we look at the rates structure of income tax and VAT. As to the pseudo-prices, reduced or free fares on the buses and trains for the elderly are an example. The redistribution effect of social security can be demonstrated by the fact that people without children are obliged to contribute to the fund that provides child benefits. Indeed some social allowances are not counterbalanced by any payment at all.

This leads on to another technique of income redistribution – the subsidizing of individuals by the government. Indeed, the revenue raised is not exclusively used to cover the cost of governmental activities; a part of it is directly passed on in cash. It is impossible to give here a complete inventory of the jungle of subsidies, rebates and allowances granted for rent and rates, to artists, to further science and research, or for many purposes. The value and the variety of these differ from government to government depending on the social priorities of the country. We set out the tax and social security systems in Britain in the next chapters, but a systematic review of all subsidies would require a study in its own right.

The redistribution has become so universal an aim in public financing that even highly technical aspects are discussed by social philosophers and idealists. Politicians, for example, appear to be very interested today in the question whether taxes and social security systems can be even more effective than they are to level out incomes, or whether this point has already been overshot. Perhaps this is a problem too serious to leave in the hands of economists. At any rate, it would be unrealistic if we tried to answer these questions without taking the unofficial economy into account.

How the citizen becomes alienated

Almost everybody agrees that a political community needs a managing body, and therefore that governments should have financial means at their disposal, but it is hard to find a person who likes paying taxes. Why is this so? It might be said that man, by his very nature, happens to be selfish and shortsighted, but this response is of little help in analysing the problem. One could just as easily point to the acts of charity or cooperation which man has achieved, in spite of his imperfections. Both statements are, of course, far too general to assist in an understanding of the phenomenon. Let us try then to be more specific.

It is the compulsory nature of taxes which is probably the most important factor in accounting for reluctance to contribute to the common till. As we have already explained, the system is what might be described as *obligatory solidarity*. Anyone who wants to buy a pound of apples has a choice of different varieties of various qualities and prices. The choice made is that which the purchaser feels is the best value for money – of taste and price. Alternatively – and this is perhaps the very essence of freedom – the would-be purchaser may eventually conclude that apples are too dear and spend the money on something else. Whatever is decided, generally speaking of course, there is no unwillingness in actually paying the agreed price, because the purchaser will be satisfied that he has got value for money. This conclusion also applies in those cases of solidarity, say lending a friend some money, or helping a local dramatic club, or supporting development work in the Third World. These are all free decisions, and few people feel inclined to shirk the financial consequences.

Naturally, all this is rather idealized. All we want to point out is how different things look when the government presents the bill for its services. There is a good reason why economists call the remainder of one's income, after deduction of taxes and social security premiums, *available* income, for indeed the part transmitted to the government is not really available; it may even be used in ways which the taxpayer does not like. Citizens may, in their most rational moments, find some solace in the idea that a democratic government's policy reflects the wishes of the majority, but there are very few people who share the opinion of the majority on each and every item of the government's programme. In reality, one taxpayer feels that the government is dealing with issues which are not its business, another thinks the government has chosen the wrong solution to problems, a third one may even deem the government's intervention detrimental. Everybody is against something, be it five or ninety per cent of government spending.

Admittedly, there are – even apart from the area of pseudo-prices – a few cases where those who do not agree can opt out. For instance, in some countries, though not in Britain, the social security laws allow for exemptions for people who have conscientious objections against insurance systems. And there are a few taxes whose proceeds are set apart for specific purposes so that you could demonstrate your disagreement with such a purpose by refusing to pay that one tax, though under the present law the deductions would eventually be made. An unwillingness to contribute to the defence budget is one of the most common cases, but whatever they are they boil down to a handful of picturesque borderline cases. The vast majority of treasury income derives from three main taxes which we shall describe in the next chapter (income tax, company tax, VAT). Their proceeds go directly to the general fund. This way of protesting is therefore seldom open to a person who objects to a particular spending item, say, expenditure on nuclear weapons. When it has been attempted and tried in the court the conclusion has been that neither the taxpayer nor the collector of taxes has the right to apportion tax revenues; this is the prerogative solely of the government.

The story, however, doesn't end there. One may

not only object to the purpose public money is spent on, but also to the distribution of the burden among the population, for instance, the form of different income tax rates at different levels of income (this concept will be dealt with in the next chapter). Here again, the coercive nature of taxes can create resentment, which prevents people from meeting their liabilities with a smile.

A second cause, strongly related to the previous one, springs from the ideas the average citizen in a modern nation intuitively has about his government. The days of the Swiss *Landesgemeinde*, where all voting members of the community came together to discuss and decide on every single matter, and then implemented the decisions themselves, or perhaps had them implemented by a few trustees chosen among themselves, are gone for ever. Modern societies are so vast and complicated that the citizen can only exert control on management through a system of representatives at national and local level. In fact, representing the people has become, at national levels at least, more or less a full-time job which can only be performed by specialist managers. This is even more so when policy decisions have to be implemented, that is management proper. As a result of these developments, Parliament and government – and, to a certain extent, their equivalents on lower levels as well – have become impenetrable mechanisms. The man in the street can change the direction at national level whenever a general election is called, but he is unable to influence the day-to-day activities of the government. Or are there still average men or women who stop to judge the size of Ms 1 and 3, the public sector borrowing requirement (PSBR), the gross domestic product (GDP) or gross national product (GNP)?

The psychological effect of the development of the modern state is an enormous gap between government and citizen. Words like 'government', 'state', 'authority', 'Downing Street', or just 'they', throw up the image of an anonymous power, a tyrant who gradually dominates life itself and imposes all sorts of unpleasant duties – taxpaying is just one of them. It seems perfectly natural that no one hands his money with a smile to such a monolithic body.

Again, sober reasoning on the requirements of modern society and the impossibility of finding an ideal solution for paying for them should help us understand why taxes have to be paid – and paid willingly. Few people seem to be able to take this attitude, however, at least permanently. Most people cooperate sulkingly at best, seeing taxpaying as throwing money into a dark hole that yields nothing, a personal loss that should be reduced if possible. And, let's admit it, we are all one of 'most people' from time to time.

The third cause of reluctance to pay is also psychological, but on a more individual level. Evading taxes can sometimes be likened to a game. Many people (not only those under twenty!) seem to enjoy, now and again, committing all kinds of petty theft. Their main incentive appears to be something more than financial benefit – it's the excitement in the risk of being caught. They steal articles of modest value from their offices, factories or from a department store, pocket the coins when a tired cashier hands them too much change, or try to get into the cinema without buying a ticket, etc. This petty thieving is particularly popular when the injured party is a branch of the authorities: re-using an unfranked stamp, having a free ride on a bus. Which of us has never done anything like that, and not felt a secret satisfaction? Some people even regret the increases in the amounts of tobacco, alcohol and other goods one is allowed to bring through the customs, because they have to forego the thrills of smuggling. The government is a nameless adversary, so 'nobody' is harmed. There is just the sweet prickling of walking the edges of peril.

A more intellectual variety of this tendency is based on smartness rather than dexterity. To cheat a policeman in order to evade a fine, or to acquire an allowance, a subsidy, on specious evidence. Here again, the satisfaction does not necessarily rest upon the financial gain, although no exact line can be drawn. However this may be, these forms of human weakness also contribute both to tax avoidance and to 'scrounging', as getting benefit payments to which one is not entitled has come to be called.

A fourth cause worth mentioning is the widely accepted view that a considerable part of our tax money is wasted, because the Civil Service perform their duties with little efficiency. This book is not the right place to discuss to what extent the service really deserves such a reputation, but it is useful to try to see it in its true proportions.

There is something unavoidable about the way expanding organizations degenerate into bureaucracy. The concept of the economics of large-scale production is taught early on to students of economics, but anyone who has had an opportunity to compare the productivity of large and small units know that this is only half the story. To be sure, there *are* economies on the technical side, but they are inevitably accompanied by complex management structures that hamper quick decision-making and by difficulties in communication, vagueness in defining the limits of particular jobs, blunting the employee's sense of responsibility, inflexibility, and all the other evils that can be looked up in any manual on industrial organization. As a rule, entrepreneurs are well aware of these hazards. Most firms try to detect and eradicate such trouble, but it goes without saying that they prefer not to wash their dirty linen in public.

A well-managed government agency will try just as hard to improve its organization, but it has less chance of keeping its weaknesses quiet. Any failure of government machinery is a public affair, as overspending is revealed in official statistics. As a consequence, the efficiency gap between a privately run unit and a government unit of the same size may appear larger than it really is. This situation has its effect on the civil servant himself. He knows that the public are watching him. In a private firm, one is not necessarily blamed for bad luck (after all, the incurrence of risks is part and parcel of entrepreneurship), but the civil servant is not forgiven for any false step. He always has to be ahead of criticism. A sailor may prefer not to go to sea when a storm is expected, a businessman similarly may prefer not to take an unnecessary risk, but, to continue the analogy, the civil servant simply dare not embark on a course of action without studying all the economic and social weather-forecasts. Excessive circumspection becomes part of his professional behaviour. He feels that his desk chair is located between the devil and the deep blue sea.

This, on its own, is enough to explain why a government is likely to function more stiffly, more bureaucratically, than a private body. Obviously, too, there is a second factor, the absence of any profit incentive. This theme is so well known that we will not elaborate on it. And we will certainly not examine whether it is fair to call this situation wasteful, that is, if there are other ways to get the jobs done. All that matters in this context is that the public believe that something is wrong, and resent it. These feelings are yet another reason for stingy and rapacious attitudes towards government.

In setting out attitudes to taxpaying, we are making no claim at all to originality. All four reasons (the coercive nature of taxation; the lack of identification with one's government; the play aspects of risk; the rancour over inefficiency in public management) have been dealt with extensively in other books. It is possible that such arguments may not even belong in an economists' book, but we believe it does no harm to mention these subjects, in order to provide some sociological and psychological background to certain aspects of the underground economy.

There is one more item, and economists are certainly qualified to discuss it, namely the level of incidence of taxes and other government levies. This is not the fifth reason for reluctance to pay; what it does is give a new dimension to each of the four. Moreover, what it does is to influence the strength of the four reasons for reluctance to pay tax. To put it even more specifically, the higher the burden of public taxes and levies, the greater will be the desire to avoid paying for any one of the reasons given. The weight of taxation and social insurance has steadily increased in the course of this century and the rate of growth is now such that the acceleration is perceptable within the span of one generation. Between 1961 and 1979, for example, national insurance contributions grew from 2.5 per cent of employees' personal income to 2.8 per cent, and personal income taxes from 9.8 per cent to 13.1 per cent.

This conclusion is, of course, only valid for the

population as a whole. These figures are certainly not contrary to the general felt impression that 'things get worse and worse'. We therefore have to be prepared to accept that the propensity to evade taxes and premiums will progress. Without any measures taken, these sources of the unofficial economy will gain in abundancy each year again.

A paradise for moonlighters?

During our research we talked to some people who we felt might be involved in the unofficial economy in some way, either on a regular or an occasional basis, as we have seen in catering. Naturally the people to whom we spoke wished to remain anonymous. In the building industry, in particular, we believe that 'black' money is of considerable significance, even though the government has taken steps to kill the 'lump'. We spoke to a part-time builder who has a regular but seasonal job at some times of the year and takes on building and painting and decorating jobs during the rest of it.

To begin with, we asked whether his regular job was enough to live on.

'In no way at all. I have a family and I have been trying to get a full-time regular job for many years. But the way things are today, it's just not possible, so I have to pick up whatever I can during the slack period.'

'Do you operate as self-employed during the lay-offs?'

'No, I can't afford to do that. Some years I don't get any work at all. At other times, there is plenty of work, so I have to get a mate to come with me, so that we can get things done on time.'

'Does that mean that you sign on the dole?'

'Of course. If it's a bad year, and I can't get any work, we couldn't survive without it. My wife goes out to work now that the children are older, but we were very short of money when they were little.'

'So at the end of the year do you tell the tax man what you've earned?'

'No, why should I?'

'Well, you do pay tax on your regular earnings, don't you?'

'Not very much – we've got four kids. After all, this is work done in my spare time. I'm giving up the time I could spend going to football or the pub: why should I pay tax?'

'Do you know that it is the law of the country that all your earnings, whether they come from your job or part-time work should be declared to the tax people?'

'Well, perhaps they should, but I can't afford to give up what I earn in extras. It's not much, but it does make the difference between the family having a holiday and not having one.'

'You don't think it's immoral not to tell the tax man about your earnings?

'Not at all. I'm not rich. Why should I pay tax? People in better jobs can do that. Tax is too high anyway.'

'So you get the dole. Do you get any other forms of social security?'

'Oh yes. We get a rate rebate and some payment called supplementary?

'But don't you think that's cheating, getting social security and earning money which you don't pay tax on?'

'Look, I've told you. When you add the whole lot up, we're not exactly living like kings, you know.'

'So how do you go about your business, putting a card in a shop window or what?'

'No. If I did that they might find out about what I earn. It costs so much money to have painting and decorating done these days. People are running after you to work for them once they know you are available. I've got some people I do a bit of work for every year. You know, one year they have the kitchen done, the next the bathroom and so on. I make them pay me cash and charge them less than a big company. A lot of them offer cash, of course, and some try to split the difference, but I'm strictly a cash man. I don't even have a bank account, so what use would a cheque be to me?'

'Do you realize that if you ran your business properly, you could charge more and get allowances for your equipment, so that even if you paid tax, you would probably earn as much in the end as you make now?'

'What, and get landed with the tax and social security people knowing all my business? Anyway, it's only a sideline for me, you know. I only do it because I have to. If only I could get a full-time job, I wouldn't do it at all. I would rather spend my spare time with my family than going out doing jobs at all hours and at the weekends too. There's more to life than work.'

'So you feel quite justified in not declaring your income?'

'I sure do! I'm not the only one doing it, you know. I've got a mate who is a plumber and he runs two businesses. One with all the bills done properly and the other strictly for cash. When I'm doing a job that needs a plumber he comes in to do it and I give him something from the money I'm getting. Of course, he doesn't tell anyone about that either. That way, he

4 Taxes: a fuel for the unofficial economy

Attempts, often successful, to avoid paying tax to which one is liable are not new: they are as old as taxation itself. They date back as far as the Romans, and medieval European monarchs were very concerned about them. In Britain, the select committees of 1851 and 1861 heard evidence on tax avoidance and others have since. In 1981, yet another House of Commons committee took evidence on the whole of the unofficial economy, tax avoidance and evasion included.

Some taxes are quite legally not paid, and to begin with it is necessary to distinguish between tax avoidance and tax evasion. The first is within the law and includes all the legal means at the disposal of an individual to reduce his or her taxes to a minimum. Just because avoidance is legal it does not, of course, follow that it is always seen as desirable or moral by society. As successive budgets have shown, Chancellors of the Exchequer are constantly bringing in legislation to stop various loopholes. As a general rule, changes are not retroactive, but if the tax-avoiding scheme is regarded as particularly reprehensible, the Chancellor and the Treasury may well decide that it must be so.

Tax evasion, in contrast, is always illegal and carries penalites. The most common form of evasion is probably not declaring income which, if declared, would be liable for tax. We can only say 'probably', because quite simply we do not know precisely, but evasion is growing and it seems likely that it probably costs the government more in lost revenue than avoidance.

What is certain is that tax evasion and avoidance together make up a large proportion of the unofficial economy in its widest sense. Although the moral implications of evasion and avoidance are different, their economic impact is the same and so to a large extent they can be lumped together in the effect they have on the official economy.

Increasingly, the two are becoming known as 'avoision' when economists assess their joint influence on society. Estimates of 'lost' revenue to the Exchequer vary enormously: the figure has been put as high as fifteen per cent of gross national product or over £20,000 million. Sir William Pile, former Chairman of the Board of Inland Revenue, suggested £10,000 million. More conservative estimates reckon it around five per cent, while others have put the figure as low as 2½ per cent of GNP. This last figure tends to be the one given out by the authorities and, it must be said, appears to have a large element of wishful thinking in it.

Professor A. L. Ilersic* has offered a figure of £7,300 million made up of tax evasion by self-employed what he calls 'fiddlers' of about £2,750 million of undeclared income by 1976–77, which he reckoned had grown to £4,000 million by 1978–79. Employed 'moonlighters', he estimated, were concealing about £2,000 million as a group, while those officially unemployed but in fact working were evading tax on around another £1,300 million, thus making up his total of £7,300. Professor

---

* *The Economics of Avoidance/Evasion*, Institute of Economic Affairs, 1979.

Illersic makes no claims that his assessment is more accurate than others. Different figures can be arrived at by using different criteria, but it is clear that whatever means are used to 'guesstimate' the figures, they are not insignificant in terms of total GNP. If tax had been paid on Professor Illersic's £7,300 million estimate at only the (in 1976–7) 35 per cent standard rate of tax, the government would immediately have a further £2,555 million in tax revenue.

In April 1981 the Association of Her Majesty's Inspectors of Taxes gave its own estimate when it was giving evidence to the Committee on Revenue Enforcement Powers. It said: 'Whether it is three per cent, 7½ per cent or more of gross domestic product is debatable, but it is clear that it is large. Both the self-employed and employees are evading tax on a considerable scale. In a perfect world no powers would be necessary but we live in a world where both petty thefts and large scale organized crime are widespread.' The association put the estimate of lost tax revenue at £4,000 million. The committee eventually announced that it felt 7½ per cent was probably the level of unofficial activity in the country.

Let us now turn to the British tax system to see how by its very nature it contributes to the growth of the unofficial economy. In the United Kingdom there are two main kinds of taxes, those which are rendered on the income and wealth of individuals or companies, and those which affect the price of goods. Income tax, whether pay as you earn (PAYE) or schedule D, the tax on dividends or interest, corporation taxes, capital transfer tax and capital gains tax all come into the first category, and value added tax (VAT) and the various customs and excise duties into the second.

All these taxes are of varying use to the government

as instruments in their economic and social policies. PAYE, for instance, which is paid by all employed persons who come into the tax levels of income, is extremely difficult to avoid for long. If tax returns are not sent to the Revenue it will issue an 'E' emergency coding, which is sent to employers. This offers only the minimum personal allowance and the employee is often therefore paying much higher tax than he need. It follows that the changing of PAYE rate can have an immediate impact on government revenue, as it is largely unavoidable. It is indeed the main source of revenue to the government.

Collecting income tax from the self-employed is more difficult. They usually put in annual accounts on income and expenditure and tax is levied accordingly. It is, however, relatively easy for them to falsify accounts by omitting cash transactions, doing business in kind with other self-employed people, employing wives or other relatives who are not really working and by exaggerating expenses like travelling and accommodation. Little wonder perhaps that successive governments have been deaf to the complaints of the self-employed at their treatment in the social security system: the unofficial view of government is that because of the very nature of their employment, their individual 'official' accounts bear little resemblance to reality. Sometimes, however, the Inland Revenue is prepared to forget about tax on the self-employed.

Perhaps one of the most scandalous instances of the Inland Revenue agreeing to forget about income tax for the self-employed was the case of the 'Mickey Mouse' Saturday night casual workers on national newspapers. For many years, these men, taken on by the unions with the agreement of the management, turned up on Saturday night, some to work and some others not. They clocked in using fictitious names like Mickey Mouse, Prince Philip, etc. and sometimes used the names of directors of the particular company. Naturally no tax was paid. In the end the Inland Revenue granted a tax amnesty in the hope that in future workmen would check in honestly. This move encouraged many other self-employed people who had not benefited from such an amnesty, to the point of a test case in the court, but the court ruled that the Inland Revenue is free in law to act in such a way if it so wished for the benefit of a certain group.

Tax on interests and dividends is also relatively easy to collect – either the company or the organization paying the interest or dividend deducts the standard rate tax before making the payment (except in some circumstances where the government allows the payments to be made tax-free).

Corporation tax, too, is difficult to evade, though in recent years it has effectively been at such a low level that there is little stimulus towards concealment in this area. Capital gains and capital transfer taxes do, of course, bring in revenue, but their main purpose is as an instrument of social policy in the redistribution of income. The temptation to avoid them is strong and it seems likely that actual yields are less than they should be, though it is impossible to assess by how much. The government has recognized the difficulty of collecting these taxes and therefore allows various reliefs which reduce the burden in the hope that most people will feel constrained to be honest.

Value added tax, which changes the cost of goods and services, is the main indirect tax and is to some extent an avoidable tax. It would be difficult to avoid paying some VAT, but for a period at least it is possible, for instance, to frustrate a government's aim of increasing its tax revenue by raising VAT. The purchase of a new car, clothes, a washing machine or pots and pans can be deferred in the hope that tax levels may come down later and, as the tax is not levied on a wide range of goods and others are 'zero-rated' so that in fact nothing is paid, it is not therefore as efficient an instrument of government policy as income tax. The same is true of customs and excise duties, particularly those on alcohol and tobacco. It is argued that increases in these taxes are part of the government's policy of reducing their consumption because of the danger they present to health. It has to be said, however, that laudable though this aim may be – if it is the aim – there would be a large hole in government revenue which would have to be filled from elsewhere were there to be a marked decline in the country's spending on drink and tobacco.

The estimates of the size of tax evasion and avoidance may well be the 5–7½ per cent of GNP as suggested by Professor A. L. Ilersic and others, but the government has no way of knowing. It is clear, however, that taxation policy is less efficient than it might be and may indeed be downright counterproductive.

Tax revenue from individuals and companies –
the main categories 1979/80

Direct taxes	£ million
Income tax	24,300.0
Corporation tax	4,645.0
Capital gains tax	508.0
Capital transfer tax	425.0

Tax revenue from individuals and companies –
the main categories 1979/80

Indirect taxes	£ million
Value added tax	8,178.6
Alcohol	2,442.4
Tobacco	2,579.1
Car tax	516.2

How taxes are levied

First of all, let us look at direct taxes. As we have said
above, the most important of these is income tax and
it is levied on all declared incomes, though some incomes may be so low as to not reach the tax threshold.
For 1981–82 the rates were as follows:

Band of income	Taxable income 1981–82
Basic rate of 30 per cent higher rate charges at:	first £11,250
40 per cent	£11,251–13,250
45 per cent	£13,251–16,750
50 per cent	£16,751–22,250
55 per cent	£22,251–27,750
60 per cent	over £27,750

In addition to these rates, there is an investment sur-
charge at certain levels on interest and dividends. It
is levied in addition to the highest income tax rate
and for 1981–82 was fifteen per cent on all investment
income over £5,500. It also applies to trusts and
settlements.

The scope of income tax is wide. Earned income
includes wages, salaries, bonus payments, benefits in
kind, business profits, pensions received by husband
and wife, share options, alimony and tips and gratu-
ities. Investment income covers dividends from stocks

and shares in public companies and interest on bank deposits, building societies, defence bonds and government stock, mortgages and loans, post office accounts and property rents. One has to ask oneself, bearing in mind the progressive nature of the tax system and the wide sweep on income liable for tax, whether people will be inclined, particularly once their income reaches higher levels, to conceal those parts of their income they can from the Inland Revenue. At the lower income levels the temptation may be to conceal a wife's earnings, if possible, to avoid tax altogether on her wages.

Against these tax rates, of course, must be set the allowances given by the government, which can lower the individual's tax bill. No one pays tax on the whole of their income, except a wife on her investment income which is aggregated with her husband's income and set against his allowances. Allowances are part of the government's social engineering to redistribute income to the needy.

Everyone gets a personal allowance (again except wives who get a wife's earned income allowance) which is fixed each year by the government at the same level and no tax is payable on incomes below that level. For 1981-2, this allowance was £1,375. Then married men got an extra £770 allowance, as did single parents of either sex, and in certain circumstances there are housekeeper, dependent relative, blind, daughter's help and age allowances. All these allowances permit people legitimately to avoid paying some tax.

There is no question of evasion here. That comes simply from not declaring all one's taxable income. There are other means of saving tax by investing in various tax-free forms of saving. These include retirement savings certificates, national savings certificates, 'save as you earn' schemes and post-war credits. Were these savings invested elsewhere, they would be taxable with a consequent gain to the Inland Revenue, so that, although they are perfectly legal and indeed desirable, they have an economic impact similar to that of not declaring certain forms of taxable income. In addition, the government permits certain benefits to be tax free. These include betting and pools winnings, cash from 'Ernie' on premium bonds, child benefit, redundancy payments up to £25,000, lump sums from an approved pension scheme, Luncheon Vouchers up to 15p a day (cash payments of 15p would be taxable), miners' coal allowance, and share incentive schemes up to £1,000 a year. Unemployment, supplementary benefits and other social security payments have been tax free so far, but the government is now planning to tax them as part of annual income, if the annual total of income and benefits is above the individual's starting level for tax.

Against all these allowances must be set some compensating benefit to the government – once again we cannot assess the amount – of extra tax paid because some people do not claim their allowance or benefits. Income tax is the government's biggest revenue raiser, bringing in £24,300 million in 1979–80, three times as much as VAT.

Corporation tax need not detain us long here. At fifty two per cent it applies only to limited companies – the self-employed pay income tax on their gross earnings, after expenses, like the employed. Small companies have a special rate of forty per cent: these are companies making profits of less than £70,000 a year with marginal relief up to £130,000. Companies can be compared to some extent with the self-employed. There will be a temptation and sometimes companies will succumb to doing as many unofficial dealings as possible, so that true profits are not revealed in the figures.

Her Majesty's Inspectors of Taxes, in a statement in April 1981 demanding more staff to stop abuses, stated that of those businesses selected for investigation by their inspectors, eighty-two per cent were found to have understated their profits. The businesses chosen were only a very small proportion of the total, 2½ per cent of non-company accounts and only a quarter per cent of companies. The additional tax recovered in the year to 31 October 1979 was £14,100,000 without recourse to interest or penalties for non-disclosure, and there was a further £40 million where interest was charged and penalties were sought. We are not suggesting here, of course, that all or even a majority of companies do this: professional auditors can usually see through this type of activity in any but the smallest companies.

Now we come to capital transfer and capital gains taxes, both to some extent voluntary taxes, as can be seen from their respective 1979–80 yields of £425 million and £508 million. The former has replaced the old estate duty which was brought in as a means of redistributing wealth on the death of a person. Capital transfer tax has the same aim, but its results are perhaps not quite so drastic, although it applies to lifetime transfers as well as those on death. Theoretically, CTT is payable on any gift, but as always with tax there are allowances and exceptions which reduce or eliminate the tax altogether.

The most important exception in CTT is that all transfers between husband and wife are exempt from tax. This means that the estate of a married couple is not taxed, as long as they leave their property to one another, until the death of the second partner. Under estate duty, each individual estate was taxed, so the estate of a married couple was taxed twice. Nevertheless, the number of tax exiles who leave the country to avoid income tax during their lifetime and CTT on their death shows no real sign of diminishing: the tax rates are clearly regarded as too high and to be avoided if possible. However; those who wish to can avoid CTT to some extent by taking advantage of the exceptions which have become increasingly generous in recent years. In any one financial year a person can transfer up to £3,000 without incurring CTT. This allowance can be used for life assurance premiums which produce tax-free yields on death, or when the policy matures. Then any number of individual gifts up to a maximum of £250 each are permitted. These, too, can be used in insurance premiums for the benefit of others.

Additional gifts may be free of tax, if a person can prove that they are part of normal expenditure and leave sufficient income for a normal standard of living to be maintained. Gifts to a bride or bridegroom up to £5,000 are allowed by parents, and elder brother or sisters, or grandparents, can give £2,500, while anyone may make a gift worth up to £1,000 without incurring tax. These allowances are intended to help people live a normal life, giving presents where they want without constantly looking over their shoulders for the tax man. The allowances can be used, however, for quite serious avoidance of CTT, serious not in any illegal or immoral sense, but in terms of reducing the final CTT which has to be paid on the estate on the death of a person. Here are the CTT current rates during lifetime and at death:

Slice of chargeable transfers £000s	Transfer on death Rate on slice % 1980–81	Lifetime gifts and transfers of small businesses and farms Rate on slice % 1980–81
0–25	0	0
25–30	0	0
30–35	0	0
35–40	0	0
40–50	0	0
50–60	30	15
60–70	35	17½
70–90	40	20
90–110	45	22½
110–130	50	27½
130–160	55	35
160–210	60	42½
210–260	60	50
260–310	60	55
310–510	60	60
510–1,010	65	65
1,010–2,010	70	70
over 2,010	75	75

This brings us to the other semi-'voluntary' direct tax, capital gains tax. In theory, this is levied on all monetary gains on any assets such as share investments, land and buildings, jewellery and antiques. But in the 1981–2 financial year, the first £3,000 of gains was exempt from the tax, so that with careful planning it is possible to avoid the tax to a considerable extent. Minor children, too, had the same £3,000 exemption. There is also a long list of exemptions to the tax, which means that apart from the very wealthy, gains tax is something many people have heard of without being subject to it. The exemptions include profits made on one's own home, the 'main private residence'. Anyone who owns more than one house must decide which one is the main residence and the other will be subject to tax, if it is sold for a profit. Any profits made on the sale of private motor vehicles is tax exempt, as is anything sold for £2,000 or less. Many government savings schemes are tax free and so are profits on British government securities which have been held for a year or more.

Other exemptions include betting or gambling winnings, compensation damages for any wrong or injury suffered, the profits on life assurance policies or deferred annuities and gifts to charities or to the nation. This brief outline shows that by taking care, the burden of capital gains tax can be substantially reduced. And quite apart from the legal means available for avoiding the tax, it is not uncommon for people to practise straightforward evasion. The reporting of profits on share dealings, for instance, is largely a matter of honour. The tax inspectors make spot checks, but it is difficult for them to find all undeclared profits, especially if the investment has been held for a short time and no dividends (which, of course, ought to be declared as part of normal income) have been paid. Where shares are bought and sold in one account – the two-week dealing period used by the stock market for settling bills – no share certificate is issued, so it is even more easy to conceal dealings. In much the same way, sales of other assets can be concealed from the tax man.

This brief outline shows how even the direct taxes imposed by the government can be mitigated by the skilful taxpayer by legal or illegal means. No tax guide exists without a section on 'tax planning' or 'tax saving hints'.

Indirect taxes

The main indirect tax levied in Britain is value added tax, commonly called VAT. It was introduced in April 1973, replacing the old purchase tax, and is levied on a wide variety of goods and services. It is a tax which is now common to all members of the European Economic Community, although the rates charged and the administration of the tax vary from country to country. Like all indirect taxes, it is voluntary. If you do not buy things or use services you do not pay the tax, which in 1979–80 raised £8,178.6 million in the United Kingdom. Similarly, those without cars do not pay car tax, and teetotallers and non-smokers escape the duties on alcohol and tobacco.

The way in which VAT is collected and the rules concerning it are enough in some cases to persuade even the most honest people to forget about it, if they possibly can. Anyone whose supplies of goods or services are less than £13,500 is not required to register for VAT; all other businesses with more than this are compelled to. This means that books must be kept especially for VAT; supplies in and out are balanced to make up the total VAT bill. Here is a simple example of how it works:

Total output of the business during the year	£80,000
VAT at 15%	£12,000
Total input	£40,000
VAT at 15%	£6,000
VAT payable (£12,000–£6,000)	£6,000

A final balance like this can be (and usually is) made up of many hundreds of small items in both directions. Many tradesmen and small businessmen are simply not up to dealing with complicated books, and VAT has meant that many of them have had to employ accountants since VAT was introduced – one could be forgiven for thinking that only accountants have benefited from the change from purchase tax to VAT, for the difference in the yield to the Revenue at various rates of tax is very small.

In Britain, VAT has been levied at several rates since its introduction, the lowest being eight per cent. At present the rate is fifteen per cent and at this level there is clearly a temptation to avoid it. It cannot be avoided where proper bills and invoices are presented, yet very few of us do not come across repeated examples in our daily lives, of statements like 'Pay me in cash and I'll charge you less', 'Make the bill half of the total and give me the rest in cash', or 'If I give you cash, will you knock something off the bill?'

One of the biggest areas of abuse is in household repairs and improvements – plumbing, decorating, electrical repairs, building, roofing and the like. These jobs are often done in spare time or at the weekends and the tax man is none the wiser. Even Sir Laurence Airey, former head of the Inland Revenue, in his evidence in May 1981 to the Commons select committee studying the unofficial economy, stated that he paid his window cleaner in cash and did not ask any questions about whether the money was declared to the tax man, though he was at pains to make it clear he was not suggesting that any illegal activity was taking place. Indeed, we must take care not to assume that simply because payments are made in cash or without bills, as can happen for jobs that involve small amounts, that all such people are dishonest in their dealings with the tax man. But it is likely that many amounts are simply forgotten about, a tendency perhaps encouraged by the relative infrequency of the issue of tax returns and visits from the VAT man. It can be seen from this brief outline that VAT and income tax are inextricably linked when it comes to tax evasion. When a job is done for cash and the worker does not declare the fee as income, the person for whom the work is done is at the same time evading VAT, so that there is a double loss to the Inland Revenue.

Perhaps the best example of the way income tax and VAT can be avoided at the same time was the practice of the 'lump', which was the term used to describe the way in which building workers avoided declaring the income from their work. At the same time, any VAT which should have been paid was avoided. The men would go in gangs to the building contractor, fix a rate for the job which was then paid in cash – and that was the end of the matter. In some cases, the men would be claiming social security as unemployed, so there was even further unlawful behaviour. Even very large companies were involved in this fraud, and during the latter half of the 1970s the directors of several companies received gaol sentences of up to five years and heavy fines. In the end a compulsory registration scheme for building workers was introduced, much against the wishes of both the workers and the employers.

Mr Roger Foster, then President of the National Federation of Building Employers, said that the scheme was 'quite out of proportion with the size of the problem' and that the 'lump' was an emotive and widely misunderstood term. Be that as it may, building workers' gangs have now been brought more effectively into the tax net, though it is impossible, of course, to catch up with those who do small jobs on their own in their spare time, with the consequent loss of income tax and VAT.

The tax avoider

When we come to look at those individuals who avoid paying tax, they tend to operate on three levels.

1 They simply avoid being taxed by, say, living abroad, having part of their salary paid abroad, not having a motor-car, keeping their chargeable assets at as low a level as possible, even perhaps rejecting a legacy. Such steps are often not feasible for private people, at least during their working lives, but they can be attractive for companies.

2 Keeping their taxation base and therefore the rate of tax charged down. There are many people who decline to do extra work or are not as productive as they might be, because they do not think the net result of their endeavours is worthwhile because of the tax charged. These people increase the more progressive the tax system is. People who behave in this way are, of course, not doing anything illegal and have no direct bearing on the underground economy. There is a link with the underground economy, however, because the high rate of tax tempts people to keep their apparent base down.

3 Treating taxation as just another personal or industrial cost and taking steps to mitigate it. Firms, in regarding company tax as a cost element, may raise prices to improve the net level of their profits. At the same time, workers may express their demands for

higher wages in take-home pay, rather than gross wage rates.

It is important, in looking at methods of avoiding tax, to distinguish between legal tax dodging and fraud. Between these two, there is a zone of semi-legal activity, where people take refuge in trusts, tax havens, disposal of assets and various other means to keep tax down. It is these loopholes, that the government constantly seeks to plug.

One of the latest moves, which involved a change in the law, was to make income from overseas trusts taxable in the hands of beneficiaries resident in Britain, following the revelation in the *Sunday Times* by Philip Knightley that the Vestey family, one of Britain's richest, had almost wholly (and legally) avoided paying tax over many years by the use of such trusts.

Then it can be said that the government positively wants some taxes to be avoided. These include tariffs on imported goods to discourage their purchase in favour of home-produced goods; possibly, though we are not persuaded of this, the taxes on alcohol and tobacco; and positive tax incentives offered to companies investing in capital equipment.

Certain activities and transactions, as we have seen, are also tax free. These include the £3,000 annual exemption on capital gains, and the various capital transfer tax allowances. Attempting to collect these taxes would be far more expensive than the yield and could well fail.

From these instances, we progress through a variety of taxes and activities relating to them where the government takes a varying view over their evasion. Here is a list of some of the maximum penalties for illegal tax dodging: they are not excessive.

Offence	Penalties
Failure to submit returns	£50 for each return, plus £10 per day after a court declaration
Failure to submit return continuing beyond tax year following that in which issued	£50 plus total tax based on return
Incorrect return	£50 plus twice the additional tax in the case of fraud and in other cases £50 plus the additional tax
Assisting in the preparation of incorrect returns or accounts	£500
Supplying incorrect information to the Revenue	£500 in case of fraud – otherwise £250
Failure to give notice of liability to tax	£100
Failure to make, when required, a return of fees, commissions, etc.	£50 plus £50 for each additional day in default
False statement made by subcontractor to obtain exemption from tax deduction	£5,500

The never-ending tug of war

Many people will never pay tax willingly, but at the same time governments need revenue to perform their task. This leads to an unending cycle of tax dodging followed by amendments in the law to plug the loophole, followed by further schemes to avoid tax, followed by yet more amendments to the law. The consequences of this cycle are undesirable: the law regarding tax has a patchwork effect and becomes a labyrinth, through which few people can find their way and the average taxpayer loses track of the main structure of the tax law. From this, it follows that the fiscal machinery can no longer cope and ensure proper maintenance of the law. A great deal of fraud goes undetected, those who do pay their taxes become resentful and, as we have seen, much tax money is lost.

The government of the day may not mind particularly, but equally it may. The powers of the tax collectors may be widened and strengthened so that there is much tighter control. The law may be applied in a stricter way. The penalties for tax offence, which are often not imposed if negotiations reach a satisfactory conclusion, could be mandatory. Few people today, for instance, pay the £50 for not filling in a tax return. The claim of an inability to do so will often be accepted by the tax inspector, who will then help the taxpayer. The imposition of a mandatory fine would not necessarily lead to greater observance of this law, but would increase resentment. The stricter the control and the higher and more complicated the tax structure, the greater will be the incentive to avoid taxation and the larger will grow the unofficial economy. As a first step in controlling the unofficial part of that economy, a simpler and less progressive tax base should be considered by governments.

A fertile ground for fiddlers

The hotel and catering trade is renowned in rumour, if not in fact, for the level of thieving and cheating which goes on. It is dangerous to assume that management is unaware of what goes on, or indeed wishes to stop it. If staff are allowed to take home bits and pieces here and there, many employers take the view that such activities enliven rather dull, low-paid jobs and enable them to keep wages down in an industry which, according to the latest estimates of the National Economic Development Office, is only thirteen per cent unionized. The tacit acceptance of fiddles can enable employers to keep the unions out, for they are only too well aware that a stronger union representation would mean much higher wages and greater job security. Gerald Mars and Michael Nicod have recently carried out detailed research in six different hotels in the Grand Metropolitan Group on the level of hidden rewards at work in the hotel industry for the Centre for Occupational and Community Research at Middlesex Polytechnic. They found that there were enormous variations from hotel to hotel in attitudes to and in the amount of fiddling, in the prevalence of it at different levels of skills, the extent to which it had been bureaucratized within the system and the level of entrepreneural 'activity', in other words, effort put in by less skilled staff to maximize their earnings by fiddling.

We have limited ourselves to talking to a small hotelier who also runs a restaurant. We turned first to his customers. We asked:

'Do customers or other outsiders come in asking for fictitious bills?'

'If they do, I don't know too much about it. I have been approached on several occasions, but I think that when people are speaking to the actual owner of the hotel or restaurant, they are careful. I don't make a great deal of money from my efforts and I'm certainly not going to help anyone to increase their income illegally in this way. It does go on I know, however, particularly in those professions where expenses get signed by superiors with few questions asked. For instance, there are many journalists who come in here entertaining one of their colleagues. That may go down on expenses as "lunch to important contact" and very few editors ask journalists to specify. If they do, journalists can fall back on their claim that they cannot reveal their sources. The same is true in advertising. But you have to remember as well that a lot of business gets done over the lunch table, or in the pub. It may be well worth paying expenses which may be something of a fiddle to get contracts. It's only a small part of the cost, after all.'

'Do you think that they then enlarge their expenses on the claim?'

'I'm sure that some of them must do, but they can pick up extra money more easily by using their own cars to travel then charging taxi or first-class train fares, or travelling second class and claiming first-class expenses. Companies know this happens, but many of them don't want to do anything about it. They realize that it's part of efficiency.'

'Now for your own business. Do you believe that your staff are getting things on the side?'

'In a business of this size, it would be difficult for them to get a great deal. We monitor our accounts carefully and watch our stock. I have to: profit margins just aren't enough in catering to operate in any other way. But in bigger businesses, it might be easier as control is more difficult. I won't say my staff don't get away with anything, but I try to keep it down as much as possible.'

'And you, what do you get in the way of tax-free earnings?'

'Well, we don't keep separate bills and only put

some of them in as our receipts to the tax man, if that is what you mean. But, of course my family manage to eat, as it were, off the menu and our own food bill is minimal. I don't regard that as cheating because we are all working in the business and we have to eat anyway. I'm not so stupid, however, as to pay more for equipment and food than I have to, and by paying cash in this area I can easily overstate expenses if I want to. The temptation is there, I must admit, but even though you are not going to print my name, I'm not going to tell you whether or not I do it.'

'Where does the better opportunity come, in food or drinks?'

'Drinks every time. I can double the amount of profit I make on a bottle of spirits by buying at one of the big discount off-licences. With food it's more difficult. You have to keep up standards or you lose customers. But it really doesn't make any difference to the quality of whisky where you buy it from. Of course, as long as you put in proper receipts and costs, there's nothing illegal, but I have to admit that this can be got round.'

'Do you get the impression that fiddling, what we call the unofficial economy, is getting larger all the time?'

'It's bound to, isn't it? Whether or not people are unfairly taxed they almost always think that they are and certainly people in business resent the VAT man. Obviously, if you can avoid all that sort of bother you will. Doing your VAT accounts isn't all that simple, you know. Small traders try to evade it if they can, not particularly because they positively want to act dishonestly, but they can't cope with the system. The same goes for income tax. Only the accountants get rich.'

'What you are saying is that the system itself promotes dishonesty?'

'Absolutely.'

'How large-scale do you think that overstating costs and understating revenue is?'

'I really couldn't say right through business as a whole. In catering, I reckon it could be up to about twenty five per cent, but I don't know. Naturally, if people are on the fiddle, they keep quiet about it for fear of being reported. Only a fool would make it public.'

'Do you think it could be stamped out?'

'Not entirely. There will always be dishonest people and, of course, always those I've mentioned who simply can't cope with the system. I suppose the authorities could be tougher, but I find them quite tough enough for me, I can tell you.'

'Do you think that people can actually lose money in the long run by not stating their profits properly? Later on, for instance, they might have to understate their losses, because they have concealed profits previously.'

'I suppose so. It seems to me that the best thing to do is to keep sensible books and not go in for large-scale embezzlement – because that's what it is, isn't it? I suspect the tax people always find you out in the end, so there's no real gain in fiddling.'

Next, we looked at the hotel and catering trade from the other side, that of the employees. Wages are low, and although managements profess that their staffs are as honest on balance as any group of workers, it is difficult to imagine even a single person living on some of the wages paid, especially those to young trainees. Without help from their parents, particularly if they are not living at home, it is virtually impossible for them to survive.

We spoke to a chef who had trained with one of the big hotel groups.

'It is the policy of most hotel groups to take in trainee chefs rather than experienced ones,' he told us. 'That way, they get cheap labour for the unskilled jobs in the kitchen at very low wage levels. As the training lasts for three or five years, a constant flow of new trainees keeps labour costs down. I remember taking home around £10 a week when I started nine years ago. I wasn't living at home, so my parents had to subsidize me. It was impossible for the first couple of years to make anything on the side, but we new boys soon caught on to what the others were doing.

'The real chance in the kitchen came when I was promoted to a junior chef. If you slice a steak carefully, for instance, you can usually get a few extra from a sirloin which you can sell to someone else in the kitchen to take home, or you can sell them cheap meals. And of course there was straightforward removal of food. I don't think any of us thought of it as stealing. Our wages just weren't enough to live on. My landlord was very keen on good food. He particularly liked chicken and prawns, so that was how I paid my rent. For several years no money changed hands at all.

'I remember one hilarious incident on the train where we had a bag full of live lobsters and crabs. One of them was very active and a claw kept appearing! One chap went out regularly with a side of smoked salmon strapped to his chest: one night he nearly got caught when he tried it with a saddle of lamb!'

This brought us to security. 'Was no attempt ever made to stop this going on?' we asked him.

'Oh yes. There were spot checks, of course, but we

always knew when these were happening. The security officers are just like anyone else, you know, they can be bribed too. They weren't getting massive wages either. There were always one or two who would warn us, in return for their share of the stuff, of course. We didn't just walk out of the door with it; there are always convenient windows to pass things through to the outside in hotels. In one hotel I was in, even the head security officer was on the fiddle. I gave him some food and at Christmas he helped me out with all my grub.

'This sort of thing goes on in all sections. Waiters, for instance, are often ordered to give their tips to the head waiter. Then it's supposed to be paid out in wages. Well, only a fool would do that, wouldn't he? The head waiters were no different from the rest of us. So normally waiters pass over only a small proportion of what they get. Not everyone takes their receipts with them, so there's quite a trade selling bills to people who can put them in as expenses.

'It's the same in the bar. Short measures are an obvious way of making money and a good barman can tell when people really don't know how much gin or whisky they are drinking. In goes the ice. Eventually it's all ice! Barmen often take in their own booze to sell to customers. The price of a bottle of gin in a hotel can be many times more than one bought in an off-licence. The barman pockets the difference. This happens in pubs, too, you know,' he added.

We know it happens, but to hear it stated so baldly nevertheless comes as a surprise. 'Surely, whatever they say, managements must accept that this happens?' we asked.

'Of course they do. They'll deny it for ever, but who can live on such wages? They say they assume parental support, but catering isn't the sort of trade where people come from rich families. And because we're working there are no grants, or anything like that. Without the perks we wouldn't be able to live. I think it's like sleeping with someone you're not married to. Your parents know that you are doing it, but they don't like you to make it obvious in front of them. Restaurant and hotel managers are the same. It's all right as long as you don't get caught.'

5 The social security jigsaw

We now turn to the social security system, which also has a large part to play in the unofficial economy, though by no means as large a part as taxation. Social security is an intermediate system between pseudo-prices (which, as we have seen earlier, are effectively nil prices) and taxes. The proceeds are allocated to specific services like unemployment pay, sickness benefit, family income supplements, rent and rate rebates, but as with taxes, affiliation to the system by means of premiums in the form of national insurance payments is compulsory, at least for those who expect to benefit should they be in need and who are employed or self-employed. To look at the social security system in this way, however, is something of an idealization, because in reality the premiums are paid not necessarily by the person insured and thus eligible for benefits, but also by employers or fellow employees. It is also true that certain social insurance funds are supplemented by the Treasury and in certain parts of the system no premiums are levied at all in a direct way.

This brings in the whole question of subsidies which are payments made by the government, which effectively reduce prices below their economic level. Examples of these include subsidized travel for the old, grants to students to enable them to continue their studies, and payment by the state of the fees of British students in their further education, grants to industries, special concessions to certain regions to encourage industrial development and a host of similar schemes.

If anything, the social security system and its administration is even more complex than the tax system. This makes its description all the more difficult, because we shall have to deal with not only the collection of money, as we did with taxes, but also its expenditure over the wide range of services. Both collection and expenditure have implications for the underground economy.

There are two main reasons for the unsystematic structure of the system. The first is that, as they do with taxes, some people cheat and try to avoid making their contributions. Moonlighters, for instance, who do not declare their income to the tax inspector, are unlikely to pay the self-employed national insurance contributions either, because that would bring their activities to the attention of the tax authorities. They may even be moonlighting and collecting social security benefits of some kind at the same time. It is not rare for a man to be collecting unemployment pay for himself and his family and to be doing a job on the side about which the authorities are completely ignorant.

Naturally, as with tax avoidance, the government tries to plug the loopholes, not always successfully. In March 1981, the government published figures suggesting that one in every twelve successful claimants for social security benefits – or over 200,000 people – got them by frauds. A report was prepared by Sir Derek Rayner who had been brought in by the Prime Minister, Mrs Margaret Thatcher, to advise the government on cutting waste. The findings in the report were based on a sample survey of social security offices which suggested that around eight per cent of claimants were receiving unemployment and supplementary benefits while they were in fact working. In the worst cases, some of the offices were said to believe that as many as thirty per cent of successful claimants had a part-time job.

Such a report was not received with equanimity, of course – particularly as it also suggested a cut in the number of jobs in social security. Many people felt that it was impossible to reach such conclusions without the evidence of a large number of prosecutions. It was also felt that, as part-time work could range from washing cars in one's spare time, babysitting, making clothes for friends, to running a painting or decorating business without declaring the income, that many activities were included which could not really be regarded as jobs at all. There is some feeling, too, that investigative powers are too wide and that they successfully attack only the most weak and vulnerable. It seems certain that the present government will continue to take a hard line. Special squads have now been introduced to stop DHSS frauds. In so-called 'non-prosecution' interviews, people sign away their rights to benefits in exchange for not facing charges.

One of the most attacked operations of benefit officers has been that of the so-called 'sex spies' who have specific instructions to question single mothers in an attempt to recoup from the putative father any benefits which go to the mother and child. A series of the most intimate questions about her sex life are asked of the mother, but it seems doubtful whether the operation is cost-effective. It costs around £6 million a year and yields about £9 million. The Department of Health and Social Security, however, justifies its actions not on the grounds of the yield, but on the principle that a man should maintain his child.

Single women and widows who may not have children but are receiving benefit have also found themselves under threat, if they happen to have a man friend. The social security office is quite likely to take the view that the man is supporting the woman even if he is not, and that he is living with her even if he is not, and stop her benefit.

Getting benefits illegally is just the same in principle as tax dodging. There is a never-ending flow of people attempting to get benefits which they think they should have, even if they are not eligible under the government's rules, pursued by the government trying to plug the loophole.

The second reason for the haphazard structure of the social security system is the fact that it has been built up gradually, paralleling changes in the views in society about the way certain groups should be protected – the workers, the poor, the young, students, the unemployed, the disabled, widows and pensioners are a few examples. As a result, new benefits have been brought in, others cancelled, changed or restructured, so that to the average person the social security is as complicated and labyrinthine as the tax system. The time has come to look at benefits in some detail.

National benefits

From November 1981, the rates for the main social security benefits which come directly from central government weekly were as follows:

	£
Retirement and widow's pensions and widowed mother allowance	29.60
Single person	29.60
Wife or adult dependent	16.30
Invalidity pension	28.35
Unemployment and sickness benefit	22.50
addition for wife	13.90
addition for each child	0.80
Maternity allowance	22.50
Injury benefit	25.25
Mobility allowance	16.50
Disablement benefit	48.30
Serviceman's disablement pension	48.50
Serviceman's widow's pension	38.45
Supplementary benefit:	
couple	37.75
long-term	47.35
single person	23.25
long-term	29.60
Heating addition:	
lower rate	1.65
higher rate	4.05
Child benefit	5.25
One parent benefit	3.30

This list is by no means the whole panoply of benefits available. In addition, there is family income supplement for those families below certain levels of income: there are health benefits, like free prescriptions, dental treatment and free milk and vitamins, housing benefits in the form of rent and rate rebates, education benefits like free school meals, uniform, education grants and fare to school, and extra help for disabled people.

Let us look at what a married man with two dependent children might receive if he is unemployed.

First of all, there is his own allowance of £22.50. To this must be added £13.90 for his wife, and 80p each for the two children, bringing his total weekly benefit to £38.00. At the same time, his wife will be receiving £5.25 child benefit for each of the children and the family will probably also be eligible for some rent and rate rebate. If they are buying a house on a mortgage, the mortgage company will probably be waiving all but the interest on the mortgage for the period for which he is unemployed. The total amount for not working, however, is by no means large enough to sustain a family and the temptation not to declare possible casual earnings, which might reduce the benefits, is clearly quite strong.

Unemployed benefits

Unemployment benefits are available to all previously employed people who have paid national insurance contributions. Today, this means virtually everyone in employment, apart from a few married women, who until April 1978 were allowed to pay only an industrial injury contribution and were permitted to continue it afterwards if they wished. From 1978 the option was not continued for women marrying after that date, and so gradually they, too, are being brought into the net of full contributions.

Signing on as unemployed has certain benefits and incurs certain responsibilities. First of all, there is the weekly benefit payment and, secondly, there is no loss of the right to any other benefits, for which those in employment are eligible. Most importantly, this means that the full rights to any state pension are preserved. In return, the unemployed person is required to visit the social security office each week to sign that he or she is still unemployed and must make him or herself available for work, if any vacancies come up. Doing a casual job, or pursuing, say, a writing career, does not necessarily make one ineligible for unemployment pay, but at the end of the tax year, the income must be declared and the tax due accordingly paid. Unemployment pay used to be tax free in any circumstances, but from now on it will be counted as total income for any one year and tax is paid if the individual's income reaches the starting tax levels after allowances. This means if a person is unemployed for three months of the year, his unemployment benefit will be added to his earned income and taxed at the end of the year. The government, too, in the Finance Act 1981, got a clause through the House of Commons saying that any tax overpaid during a period of employment would not be repaid by the Inland Revenue until after the end of the tax year, or until the recommencement of employment, so that any tax due on unemployment benefits could be duly balanced out. Both these decisions were not welcomed by the unemployed and seem likely to increase the efforts individuals make to get the best of both worlds and maximize their combined income and benefits.

Supplementary benefits

Supplementary benefits are often described as the 'safety net' of the social security services. They are available to everyone who is not working full-time and whose income falls below a certain level which is set by the government each year. There are certain rules about qualifying, as there always are, but anyone who has a shortfall in income below the supplementary level is entitled to have it topped up. Originally, there was a considerable degree of discretion allowed to the social security officers when supplementary benefits were awarded and some of them remain, but many of the discretionary rules have now become law. The unemployed automatically get the supplementary benefits as set out in the table, but those who are employed in any way face a means test. The rules are complicated and this is not the place to go into them in detail, but they include definitions of part-time work (which is less than thirty hours, or thirty-five for anyone disabled); a requirement that the applicant is signed on for work at the social security office; rules about couples – married or living together (benefit is always conditional on the man being available for work and couples are still entitled if the woman works full time); students, strikers (who may not be able to claim); absences from the country; and aliens and immigrants.

There are also rules about who can be claimed for by the man and regulations about making a claim. It must, for instance, be in writing. There will be a follow-up interview and a variety of documents can be demanded by the DHSS. The amount of benefit allowed is worked out in three steps. Firstly, normal requirement is calculated. This is the amount one needs to survive on and will include heating and lighting, clothes, fares, food, etc. Secondly, any additional requirements a particular family may have are worked out and, thirdly, housing costs. When this is completed, the social security officer will work out the level of benefit allowed and this will vary, depending on whether one is single or married or has children, and there is a difference between the ordinary rate and the long-term rate. As with unemployment, anyone who is unscrupulous may be able, in certain circumstances, to understate his resources, or overstate his needs. For instance, it is perfectly possible to be a low earner but rent a room off in one's home without declaring the rent as income.

To overcome this, the government has issued rules about calculating income or total resources. The law is quite clear. Resources are divided into two parts – income and capital. Income is money which comes in from earnings, bonus, maintenance payments and benefits. Benefits, in this case, include any of the items set out in the table (page 92).

Earnings are not counted in full as income. The benefit officer will subtract any expenses in relation to work including national insurance contributions, travel expenses, any child care costs and 15p towards a meal at work. Then £4 is 'disregarded' for the man (or single woman) and £4 for his wife or woman he is living with, while single parents have half their earnings between £4 and £20 disregarded. There are special rules for a number of earnings including things like foster child fees, trade disputes, and seasonal workers. Income tax refunds are treated sometimes as income and sometimes as capital.

Capital includes savings, property and lump sums, payments like redundancy payments. Anyone is allowed to have £2,000 in capital without entitlement to benefit being affected. It is quite easy to overcome the £2,000 limit as well, if capital can be distributed among trusted friends or relatives, so that the entitlement to benefit is not lost. In calculating capital, one's home is ignored, if one is a house-owner, but savings certificates, shares, money in trust, land, premises which one does not occupy, and lump sum payments are all treated as part of capital.

Family income supplement

Family income supplement is similar to supplementary benefits, but it is applied to people on low incomes who are in full-time work, rather than the unemployed or those who are in part-time work. Anyone who qualifies for family income supplement automatically similarly qualifies for a wide range of health benefits like free prescriptions and free school meals. Anyone is technically eligible for FIS, married or single, who has at least one dependent child and is in full-time work, either in one or more jobs. As with supplementary benefits, where FIS is applied to a couple only the man can be counted as the head of the household. This means that if the man is unemployed and the woman working full-time, the family is not eligible for FIS, but must claim supplementary benefit instead. All children under sixteen, or over if they are still in full-time education, are eligible for FIS, if they live in the family home. The self-employed are also eligible, if they are employed for more than thirty hours a week.

The level of FIS is worked out in a similar way to supplementary benefits, though there are certain differences and the level varies depending on whether the claimant is single or married and how many children there are in the family. As with other benefits, the level is set by Parliament each year.

Health benefits

There are a number of health benefits, which are not means-tested. Free prescriptions are available to men over sixty-five and women over sixty, to expectant mothers, people suffering from chronic illnesses and those already receiving supplementary benefit or FIS. On a slightly different basis, free dental treatment, dentures and glasses of free milk and vitamins for children are also available.

Housing benefits

Rate and rent rebates are worked out according to income, but it is possible to have quite a high income and get a contribution towards housing costs. Normally, only tenants and householders can claim, and rent rebates are allowed to council and new town tenants. Those renting private accommodation receive instead a rent allowance, at the same level, and the premises can be furnished or unfurnished. Rate rebates can be claimed by owner occupiers, council and private tenants. First of all, the local authority will check the applicant's needs, allowances, which is at a rate set for single people, couples, and dependent children. Next, the weekly gross income is calculated. This includes income from all sources including child benefits, FIS, supplementary benefits, etc., with certain exceptions, including mobility allowances, maintenance payments and any tax rebates.

Then the rent and rates paid is averaged out over fifty two weeks, and the following formula is applied:

If income is equal to the needs allowance:

Rent	Rates
rebate equals 60% of rent	rebate = 60% of weekly rates

If income is less than the needs allowance, the rebates are raised:

Rent	Rates
rebate/allowance = 60% or rent + 25% of the difference between income and needs allowance	rebate = 60% of weekly rates + 8% of difference between income and needs allowance

If income is more than the needs allowance, the rebates are less:

Rent	Rates
rebate/allowance = 60% of rent – 17% of difference between income and needs allowance	rebate = 60% of weekly rates – 6% of difference between income and needs allowance

This brief sketch shows the wide range of benefits available to those on low incomes, or unemployed. They are never enough to enable the really impoverished to live as well as they could, if they were in jobs paying average wages or more, but they are to some people – and we are not suggesting that it is a great number; we accept the eight per cent suggested in Sir Derek Rayner's report – a temptation to fiddle. Social security 'scroungers' do not contribute as much as tax dodgers to the black economy, though it must be remembered that tax dodging and fiddling social security may both be practised at the same time by some people. And once again, we must recognize the balancing item of those people who do not seek benefits when they are eligible, though we have no means of knowing how large that figure is either.

There are clearly connections between social security payments and taxes in the underground economy. On the one hand, both systems can be described as the gateway to the unofficial economy. On the other hand, both are important tools in any government's policy, whether these may be the furthering of its social aims, defending its country from attack, providing education, policing services, and the like. It is clear from our study of both the tax and social security systems that their efficiency as government tools is jeopardized by the existence of the underground economy.

When considering tax and social security as the gateway to the underground economy, one is tempted to think exclusively of 'black' money. This is an oversimplification, for 'black' money arises through other activities, too – criminal acts such as theft and fraud are examples. Conversely, social security benefits paid out on false claims swell the size of the underground economy, but they are not strictly speaking 'black' money. What is clear, however, is that the tax and social security systems have given rise to a host of operations which are legal but distort official statistics.

As to the efficiency of the system, there is no doubt that social security benefits are simply instruments of government policy. That is the very reason they were introduced in the first place. Several characteristics of the payments system confirm this; the compulsory nature of affiliation for all employees, the compulsory payments by employers and the relation of the pre-mium to the individual's income.

Taxation, too, is also a policy tool and not just a matter of raising funds for the government. The progressive nature of the tax system is designed to re-distribute income. Tax policies towards children are also an excellent medium for redistributing wealth. The tax levels have implications for prices, employ-ment, the pact of industrialization and even for social policies, such as the health considerations in the taxes on tobacco and alcohol.

Double dealing in antiques

'You might call this little house the fruit of my immoral earnings,' said the British antique dealer we talked to in France. 'I certainly could not have afforded it in the ordinary way of business, if I declared all my dealings to the tax man. Of course we in the antiques trade don't talk about it, but we are all at it.

'Antique dealing is not flourishing in the economic conditions we have in Britain right now, so I have to try to make something on the side. Naturally the dealings and profits which I hide are not the bulk of my business – far from it – but they are the icing on the cake. I have my shop, which runs on quite expensive furniture, and on the whole my books are quite normal there. If someone comes in and doesn't want a receipt, or wants the bill made out lower than the price, I don't see why I shouldn't do it. Foreigners particularly like understated bills, so that they will not have to pay as much duty if their country happens to charge it on old stuff. I can easily replace my stock by paying cash for something similar, so there is no need for the transaction to go through the books.

'Then I have my stall in an antique supermarket where I sometimes do really well, because the trade is much more casual. Very often in the holiday season or before Christmas people are rushed and don't ask for bills and I have quite a lot of small priced stock there which has never gone into the books. If they want a receipt I simply mark it in and out again after I've sold it. In my trade, too, there are often interchangeable stock items, so I don't run much risk of being caught.

'A lot of stuff goes through my business as if it had never been there. I go to auctions and pay cash whenever I can to avoid complicated bookkeeping. I also go to markets like the one in Bermondsey in London. If you know what you are looking for, you can pick up bargains for cash and sell them for cash, perhaps repaired a bit, at a profit you don't need to tell anyone about.

'Early on, I decided that if I could do repairs to furniture I could maximize my profits, so I learned polishing and all that, and I'm not bad at upholstery either.'

After talking to several people about their unofficial dealings, one tends to become quite blasé about the subject, but the thoroughness with which people will pursue illegal activities which are quite small and often unnecessary, as they are losing out on quite legitimate business expenses and running the risk of prosecution, can be quite breathtaking.

We asked the dealer if she did not think that all this kind of trading was dishonest and whether she really knew that it is against the law not to declare income and profits and then pay the tax due on them. Was she aware, too, of all the concessions made to small businesses, which mean that taxwise they are much better treated than people on PAYE?

'I suppose the government might take the attitude that I am a minor criminal, but I don't see it that way. Things have been bad for us since VAT was introduced. As you know, purchase tax was not payable on second-hand stuff and the imposition of VAT hit us hard. Not only did the price of everything we sold have to go up to allow for it – and make no mistake, fifteen per cent is a killer – but those of us who are no good at maths have to have someone in and pay them to do the bloody VAT forms.'

We replied that for someone with no head for figures she seemed to be doing quite well.

'Yes, but that's not being good at sums or with money: thats just looking after number one, and it's what I do.'

6 Measuring the unofficial economy

We now come to the size of the unofficial economy, a subject of long and intense speculation which cannot really lead to anything more than estimates, for by their very nature they are activities which people are reluctant to reveal. What economists are generally trying to work out is the actual amount of 'black' money in circulation – money which arises through failures to declare income, or overstating expenses, or money which arises through downright dishonest activities like shoplifting, burglary, or pilfering from shops, factories or office premises by employees.

We will rely on previously published work to examine in this chapter whether parts of the unofficial economy can be expressed in figures. First a few general points before we move on to the British economy in detail.

It is arguable that both the unofficial economy and its 'black' component have been systematically underestimated, until recently, in their significance and size. The response to the first publication on the subject by one of us in Holland in 1974 and then again in 1976 showed that people thought the figures exaggerated. The Central Statistical Office in Holland initially dismissed the suggestion that it should investigate the size of the unofficial economy. The government also believed at first that it was only a minor phenomenon that did not have much impact on the overall economy. Recently, people have come to realize that this is not so, but many still think that it is smaller than was suggested. Government investigations in Holland have so far been limited to cases of tax evasion. It seems that the Dutchman's traditional enterprising spirit has found a fertile ground in the field of the unofficial economy. The way 'black' money is raised by tax evasion and other methods does indeed have some characteristics in common with typical entre-preneurial activities: one takes a risk and one is re-warded for it, or alternatively a loss is sometimes made.

Much the same applies to the United Kingdom. It cannot be said that successive governments here have ignored the phenomenon, as parliamentary commit-tees have taken evidence on it for more than a century, but official estimates seem to err on the low side.

Economists, too, have been slow to realize the im-portance of the unofficial economy. Hidden produc-tion has hardly been studied at all, and attempts to establish true income distribution have been just as few. Admittedly, these are not easy tasks, but the time has come to examine all aspects of the unofficial econ-omy, even though it may not be possible to quantify each of them.

One of the reasons for the systematic underesti-mation of the unofficial economy is that economists often deal with theories based on the global models we discussed earlier, sometimes forgetting to pay enough attention to what is really happening in busi-nesses and households. Also, the whole subject of the unofficial economy is still taboo to some extent, be-cause it implies that much of what has been accepted as reliable statistical data is untrue, or less true than supposed.

The size of the unofficial economy can, of course, only be estimated and it is important to recognize that it cannot be expressed in a single figure. The phenomenon has many different aspects, including hidden income, hidden employment and hidden unemployment. Let us take income distribution, which is 'askew' because some incomes are high and others low, some work pays less than others and women still often earn less than men. The question is how the official picture is affected by hidden incomes and whether these represent an equalizing factor to some extent or not. The true extent of the 'skew' in the national income distribution can be decided only when we have the answer to this question.

Another striking aspect of the unofficial economy is hidden employment and hidden unemployment. When looking at these, we can estimate the figures involved and compare them with those published every month by the Department of Employment and the Department of Health and Social Security. This will produce yet another estimate for the size of the unofficial economy.

The next aspect of the unofficial economy is hidden production. This is difficult to determine, since it includes invisible production in the form of commercial transactions. One needs to know whether a tradesman uses invoices, buys legal or illicit goods and materials, and whether his activities involve a change of ownership of goods, which is the criterion of productive transactions. There are, of course, no figures for the number of transactions with or without invoices and about the number of illicit transactions. A survey among firms and households might throw some light on this matter, but the reliability of the answers given would depend on the respondents' honesty. The same difficulties arise when we want to estimate, for example, the extent of private domestic help, or unofficial production in the building industry. The answer in each case will depend on which aspect (income, work or production) we bear in mind.

In April 1981, Bruno S. Frey and Hannelore Weck of the Institute for Empirical and Economic Research at the University of Zurich produced a paper, *Estimating the Shadow Economy: A 'Naïve' Approach*, in which they discussed the problems of estimating the size of the unofficial economy and those aspects of society which lead to it, in which they included taxation, where they ranked Britain the tenth most heavily taxed nation after Sweden, Norway, the Netherlands, Denmark, Belgium, Austria, Germany, Finland and France. Weighting together taxation and legislation, they put Britain fourth highest in terms of the shadow economy after the Netherlands, Denmark and France. The problem, they found, was that estimates of the level of the unofficial economy varied enormously depending on the criteria used. Taking taxation and regulation, for instance, it appears that Italy has a very small unofficial economy, whereas in fact the country is rumoured to have a high one. So much must depend on just how willing people are to evade taxes. On that precept, more people in Italy are prepared to avoid paying their taxes than elsewhere. On this basis, the Swiss are the most moral nation in the world, though they are not at the bottom of the taxation league.

In the end, one has to try to balance the taxation burden, the effectiveness of legislation and regulation and the individual's attitudes towards paying tax (which might be described as 'tax morality') and their understanding of the system, coupled with the impact of the labour market and available jobs. Using all these barometers of possible unofficial activity, Frey and Weck reached a conclusion on which countries would have shadow economies which were 'very large', 'large', 'small' and 'very small' in relation to officially measured GNP. They did not attempt to quantify these, for they felt that estimates already made did not always square up with the estimates given for different countries. For what it is worth, however, this is how they ranked various countries:

Size of unofficial economy	
Very large	Netherlands
	Belgium
	Austria
Large	Italy
	France
Inconclusive (depending on how you measure unofficial activity)	Canada
	Sweden
	Denmark
	Norway
	Ireland
	Germany
	Spain
Small	United Kingdom
Very small	United States
	Finland
	Japan
	Switzerland

This conclusion contrasts sharply with that of Edgar L. Feige who tried to estimate the level of the unofficial economy in the USA ('How Big is the Irregular Economy?' *Challenge*, November/December 1979).

Feige first assumed that the total economic activity in a country is reflected in the total volume of financial

The greater increase in item 1 could be due to a change in prices, but Feige said that this effect would make the ratio decrease, for if prices go' up, more money is needed for financing the same economic acitivites. He found that if price indices are used (which give the change in prices with respect to the previous year), prices dropped if incomes between 1939 and 1978 were compared. He concluded that the increase in the ratio between 1 and 2 (that is, between the money involved in financial transactions and the national income) must have been due to an increase in the unofficial economy.

To determine the size of the unofficial economy, Feige started by saying that, in the absence of an unofficial economy, the ratio between the value of transactions and the national income, 10:30 for 1939, should also apply to 1976 and 1978 if there had been no development of the unofficial economy. He found the value of the national income that would give a ratio of 10:30 in each of these two years, and subtracted it from the official figure for the national income. Feige equated the remainder, that is the extra income, with unofficial income, the extent of which he estimated was 19 per cent for 1976 and 26 per cent for 1978 under the following column headings, in thousand million dollars: total value of all transactions; estimated national income; official national income; unofficial national income; and unofficial income as a percentage of estimated national income.

According to these figures, 19 per cent and 27 per cent of the entire US economy was accounted for by the unofficial economy in 1976 and 1978 respectively. In other words, the economic transactions in the unofficial economy amounted to nearly 22 per cent and to about 33 per cent of the calculated gross national product in 1976 and 1978. The figures also show that the unofficial economy increased from 1976 to 1978 by 91 per cent, while the official national income increased by 23 per cent in the same period. Feige then began to examine the unofficial British economy with equally interesting results, as we shall see.

The unofficial economy in the UK

Let us now turn to the more detailed estimates we have of the size of the unofficial economy in Britain. We must emphasize of course that they are only estimates, and may have large errors, but broadly the evidence which is available is as follows:

1 The amount of money held in cash has increased sharply in Britain in recent years. It is difficult to put any precise estimate of growth on this, because the picture varies enormously depending on the base rate chosen, and inflation anyway accounts for some of the increase.

2 There has been a growth in the number of bank notes people carry, particularly larger denomination notes. In 1970 only ten per cent of notes were in £10 and £20 denominations: by 1980 the figure was fifty per cent. This is also an unreliable method of calculating growth, as £20 notes were only introduced in 1970 and again inflation could account for a good part of the growth.

3 The ratio of currency to current accounts increased in the period from 1960 to 1975. This increase is not remarkable and is only of minor significance.

4 There have been changes in the gap between national income and national expenditure. There would be no unofficial economy if these two figures

tallied, and they never do. Some small gap is inevitable, but, as we have seen, a wide or increasing gap is strong evidence of the existence of a 'black' sector in the economy. We will look at these estimates in more detail later.

5 There is anecdotal evidence such as we have collected in this book and has been collected by others. The widespread nature of tax evasion in Britain and the way in which such actions are accepted by a large section of the population suggests a comparatively large 'black' sector. This is backed up by the guess of Sir William Pile, former Chairman of the Inland Revenue, in March 1979, that it was possible that income not declared for tax purposes could be as much as 7½ per cent of GNP. In August 1980, Sir Laurance Airey, the new Chairman of the Inland Revenue, repeated this figure to the Parliamentary Public Accounts Committee. He reasserted the claim in July 1981, following suggestions in the annual Treasury *Blue Book* that the figure was more like 2½ per cent. Backing for the anecdotal evidence has come from the Inland Revenue Staff Association, which has stated that four out of five companies 'understate' their profits, that £1,000 million tax is 'outstanding' on Schedule D, and that £120 million has been deducted from employees under the PAYE scheme and not returned to the Revenue.

6 Figures from researchers into the unofficial economy.

Before looking at the available statistical evidence, there are some general points to be made, for as we have said before, the unofficial economy is made up of several economic phenomena.

Hidden production

Officially earned money, that is, income which is declared to the Inland Revenue and will be taxed accordingly, implies official transactions.

If goods delivered or services rendered are not recorded, this means that the money involved disappears from the official statistics, and productive activities remain unnoticed. In other words, the official figures for gross national product (GNP) are inevitably incorrect.

Transactions remain hidden when they feature on invoices only in part or not at all. Everybody involved in the unofficial economy is productive, but his or her output is not included in the official figures. For example in the hotel, entertainment and restaurant sector, part of the production takes place in the field of the unofficial economy. The tax man may receive a figure for the number of meals served, but restaurant entertainers may not declare their income at all, or only a small amount, so that their output is not recorded in official figures. Much has already been said in this book about hidden output in the building industry. Doctors, dentists and consultants do more work than the official figures suggest. The part-time jobs of school-children and college students also effectively contribute to production and may not be recorded. The same goes for shopkeepers who shut their tills an hour before closing their shops: this gives them a hidden turnover and amounts to hidden output. The work of prostitutes is productive in the economic sense, but does not lend itself to auditing. In Britain we have seen that the Inland Revenue does not *want* to record it. In the transport sector, too, more is produced than is known officially: cab drivers can make more trips than are shown on the cab meter, and lorry drivers can work overtime that does not show up anywhere. There are, no doubt, many other examples.

There are, of course, different ways of looking at these cases, and it should not be assumed that every doctor, prostitute, cab driver, singer, shopkeeper or student contributes to production in this way. What concerns us is only the distortion of the official picture. If we include unrecorded production, the figures for the national product will look different, perhaps, in fact, better: maybe we are better off than we realize. The drastic abolition of all this hidden output would probably be disastrous for the country.

Hidden unemployment

Hidden unemployment arises when people are officially registered as employees but, in fact, have no work. This situation can distort the official unemployment figures, and social legislation is such that this does actually happen. In the latest government estimates, hidden unemployment or false claims for benefit affected about 200,000 people. There is no doubt that legislation for the disabled means that fewer are shown as unemployed than there really are.

Hidden jobs

It is those jobs for which people get paid but which are not reported to the Inland Revenue that constitute the major part of tax evasion. The Outer Circle Policy Unit organized a seminar in March 1980 on 'The Hidden Economy'. From this seminar a number of points arose which illustrate the difficulties faced in assessing the size of unofficial dealings in Britain. They are worth setting out for they show the difference in attitudes to evading tax on income and the problems in measuring it:

1 Tax evasion, let alone the 'hidden economy', appears in a different light to different people. Tax officials necessarily have a view which does not accommodate the positive aspects of tax evasion perceived by some economists and sociologists.

2 Tax evasion is substantial, but no measurements are likely to be forthcoming sufficiently persuasive to produce any radical change in tax policy. Scepticism was certainly expressed about any macro-measures of tax evasion: patient investigation at a micro-level might yield some more convincing estimates and work of this kind is being pursued at the Institute of Fiscal Studies.

3 Tax evasion confers benefits unequally, but although there is a strong feeling against large-scale fraud, most tax evasion is on a small scale and is not held to be morally obnoxious even by the majority of those who do not benefit; and many people cannot see any moral difference between avoidance and evasion. While most instances of tax evasion may be small, we do not know whether they constitute a greater loss to the revenue than the smaller number of large evasions.

4 Many of the practices which result in tax evasion are of long standing and built into the structure of rewards of particular industries and are not likely to vanish as a result of more enforcement.

5 There are in any case uncovenanted benefits from tax evasion which can easily be overlooked and ought to be taken into account in any calculation

of the benefits of stricter enforcement. The authorities have, of course, to make some estimate of the balance between the costs of enforcement and increased revenue. The point here is a wider one: stricter enforcement, besides generating hostility, may cut off activities which are on balance beneficial to society as a whole. This possibility needs further investigation.

6 Some proposals to mitigate the 'unforeseen' effects of enforcement, such as exempting small businesses from various forms of taxation (e.g. national insurance contributions) might result in new forms of evasion, such as the bogus registration of companies, as has happened extensively in Italy. Experience generally suggests that taxpayers are ingenious at adapting their affairs to take advantage of exemption. It might, as an alternative, be worth experimenting to see whether schemes, such as increasing workers' control of their jobs, would help to lessen the non-monetary incentives for evasion.

7 The most straightforward proposal for eliminating the bulk of evasion is to raise tax thresholds. This would be expensive, and would require a major overhaul of the system of personal taxation, which may be desirable on other grounds. It would, in particular, be worth examining a simplification of the system, even at the price of abandoning the elaborate measures aimed at securing equity between taxpayers, since these provide both the opportunity and the incentive for abuse.

8 In the meantime, the Inland Revenue and Customs, subject to political, administrative and resource constraints, mount a continuous search and destroy operation against successive targets whether large-scale frauds or widespread practices in particular

industries. It is a question whether these operations are not more cost effective than similar exercises against social security fraud.

Hidden income distribution

All hidden economic activities provide an income one way or another, and this affects the income distribution of the country, even though it is difficult to establish how and to what extent. For example, the fringe benefits of top management in both the private and the public sector (such as cars with or without chauffeurs, free telephones at home, business lunches and entertainment, even clothing allowances) push these people into a higher income group than is at first apparent, but it is difficult to quantify the effect of these allowances. Some people in lower income groups may also get a substantial extra income in a more direct way: free fares for railway workers, free coal for miners, or permission to remove products from factories. When the unofficial economy is taken into account, the national income distribution is still askew, but possibly in a different way from that indicated by the official statistics.

The distribution of income and its redistribution have been a subject of intense debate in the United Kingdom. It is impossible to quantify in any meaningful way the extra income people get throughout the various levels of society. The opportunities for adding to one's income in an unofficial way vary from trade to trade and from profession to profession, and individuals differ in the extent to which they are prepared to take part in the unofficial economy. It is relatively easier for professional people to get added tax-free perks to their income than it is for civil servants, so the latter put up a genuine fight for a bigger slice of the national income. It is no use telling them that they have index-linked pensions and private people do not, because that is a benefit they may or may not pick up at a later date.

Let us say we put hidden output at ten per cent of the national income, what does that mean? There may be fringe benefits to higher income groups, like expense accounts and pretending that a private expense has been incurred for a business purpose; some unofficial income may go abroad and create even more income in the form of interest. The lower paid, in contrast, may get free food, transport or fuel.

We cannot even assume that the extra ten per cent is distributed evenly throughout society and therefore has a uniform effect. Such an assumption would not hold water: there are groups of people who have no access to unofficial income, and they may be the majority of people. This may mean that those who are already overtly well-off may be, in fact, more wealthy than they appear, or that those who seem to be at the bottom of the economic heap are not doing to badly after all. Whether the unofficial income in society has a levelling effect, or the opposite, depends on which income groups derive the most benefit from unofficial opportunities.

Hidden consumption

It is astonishing that, though Britain is going through a recession, there are no overwhelming signs of it around us as we learn from the news, economic indicators and government publications. In fact, if one looks around in the street, one may get the impression that people are better off than before. One reason is that fortunately the welfare state makes sure that un-employment does not cause dire poverty as it did in the 1930s. But it is still surprising that, despite reports of a very poor business situation, individual consumption has continued rising in recent years and the hiccups in growth are small and only temporary.

The statistical evidence

Let us look now at the article in *Economic Trends* (February 1980) where Mr Kerrick Macafee of the Central Statistical Office set out his conclusions on the size of the unofficial economy in Britain. In his article, Macafee listed his definition of what could and could not be included in the unofficial economy:

Summary description of the household, formal and hidden economies

Type of personal gain	Whether part of hidden economy	Some examples (including some types which may belong to more than one category)
A Working for no remun-eration, often thereby avoiding paying others to carry out the work concerned.	No. This is outside the boundary of production. It is termed here the household economy.	Housework, DIY, gardening, voluntary charity work, lift-sharing.

Summary description of the household, formal and hidden economies

B Working for money, fully declared as necessary to the Inland Revenue.	No. This is termed here the formal economy.	PAYE earnings, etc.
C Enjoying a personal benefit and possible tax advantage from 'expense account living', etc.	Yes.	Enjoying five-star accommodation when conducting important business abroad on behalf of employer.
D Receiving remuneration of goods or services greater than their valuation for tax purposes.	Yes – to the extent undervalued.	Fringe benefits.
E Illegally submitting an incorrect or insufficient tax declaration.	Yes.	Undeclared income from second job. Self-employed undeclared gross income or overstated expenses. Undeclared earnings, e.g. tips. Company tax evasion.

		Some undeclared barter transactions. Undeclared earnings gained when 'unemployed' or 'sick'.
F Frauds connected with the production of goods and services in the formal economy (not exclusively related to tax fraud).	Yes.	Office pilfering. Fiddling of customers or employers by employee. Employment of employees 'off-the-books'. Shoplifting.
G Undeclared criminal or immoral earnings.	Yes, in principle.	Drug-trafficking. Prostitution.

We will not repeat all his arguments here, but suffice to say that he maintained that the largest part of the hidden economy was incomes not declared for tax purposes and probably amounted to 3½ per cent of gross domestic product:

£ million	1972	1975	1978
Self-employment income	410	1,720	2,760
Wages and salaries	100	320	850
Company profits	25	25	25
All evasion	540	2,070	3,740
GDP (I) at factor cost	54,950	192,610	140,930

As a percentage of public item

Percentage			
Self-employment income	8.0	19.0	21.0
Wages and salaries	0.3	0.5	1.0
Company profits	0.3	0.2	0.1
All income	1.0	2.2	2.6
Initial residual difference as % of GDP (E) at factor cost	1.4	3.6	3.3

(I) income, (E) expenditure.
Source: *Economic Trends*.

The whole of the hidden economy of course is rather larger than this, though Macafee does not think that the illegal aspect, at least, is substantially more. His figures suggest that the long-term movements in the initial residual difference showed that the hidden economy has grown over the past twenty years, but not in a spectacular way. As the table shows, there appeared in fact to be a fall between 1975 and 1978, though between 1972 and 1975 the initial residual difference almost doubled. This estimate cannot be compared directly with the 7½ per cent offered by Sir William Pile, former Chairman of the Board of the Inland Revenue. The national accounts take note of other types of missing income as well as tax evasion. They include, for instance, lower tax revenue because of legitimate tax avoidance, and concealed transfer payments that may be liable for tax but do not affect the measurement of GNP.

Macafee feels that none of the measurements used to try to assess the size of the unofficial economy are really satisfactory. The initial residual difference has the obvious defect that it does not represent fully all unrecorded income. The theory, especially popular in the United States, that the more cash there is in circulation the bigger the unofficial economy, is not wholly reliable either. Macafee notes: 'in the United Kingdom, it has been estimated that the amount of notes in circulation was equivalent to about £200 per adult in 1979. Certainly the level of cash in circulation has fallen less than might have been expected given the steady increase in payments for goods and services by bank cheque and credit card transactions. In recent years the number of high denomination notes in circulation has risen more sharply than a simple comparison with inflation would suggest (£10 and £20 notes accounted for 24 per cent of the value of notes in circulation in February 1976 and for 48 per cent in February 1979) and this has been cited as evidence of a mushrooming hidden economy.'

Macafee feels that the changes are difficult to assess and do not necessarily indicate such a growth: 'The United Kingdom has had a history of paying employees in cash and many covert transactions can be conducted using open cheques or even crossed cheques especially if second bank accounts are employed. The Bank of England consider that the recent increases in the circulation of higher denomination notes are consistent with the public's tendency to economize on the number of notes they carry. The number of notes in circulation varies inversely with the average denomination. Concrete instances of the increasing use of notes of higher denomination in quite open transactions are the agreements between employers and trade unions to include £10 notes in wage packets. Even so the circulation of higher denomination notes would need to have risen faster than it did for the average denomination to have kept pace with inflation. The problems surrounding the interpretation of movements in the amount and type of cash in circulation suggest that this cannot be a reliable method of measuring the hidden economy.'

Similarly Macafee believes that attempts to assess the hidden economy by turning to the Family Expenditure Survey are unsatisfactory. The income and expenditure data does not cover the same periods, the income data, especially for the self-employed, is subject to respondent and non-response errors, and it is unlikely that any proper estimate of the size of the criminal economy can be made at the present time, because statistics published by the Home Office for fraud and theft are dependent on victims' reports and understate the level of crime.

Macafee believes, however, that more information is possible on the hidden economy and suggests three other areas of promising research:

'a. A thorough study of the initial residual difference in order to confirm that the increase in its size in recent years has been primarily due to an increase in concealed income rather than for any other particular reason.

'b. A specialized expenditure survey concentrating on transactions thought to be imprecisely recorded by the Family Expenditure Survey. This would include payments for house repairs and other jobs, with a special emphasis on work paid for in cash on the understanding that other forms of payment would entail a higher price.

'c. A long-term, in-depth study of the incomes of persons likely to be concealing income. This type of survey will have to be carried out by experienced, non-government researchers who would need both patience and skill in order to gain the trust of their interviewees. There is no easy method of confirming anecdotal evidence that some workers conceal large parts of their income.'

The O'Higgins view

In a background paper for the OCPU seminar, Mr Michael O'Higgins, of the Centre for Fiscal Studies at the University of Bath, set out his estimates of unrecorded income using the Macafee figures and also a conversation he had had with the Central Statistical Office in April 1980.

Estimates of unreported income, 1972 and 1975 and 1978.

	£ million			
	Self-employment income	Wage and salary income	Company profits	Total
1972	410	100	25	540
1975 Estimate B	1,720	320	25	2,070
1975 Estimate C	1,150	320	40	1,510
1978 Estimate B	2,760	850	25	3,640
1978 Estimate C	2,150	800	80	3,030

	As percentage of published item		
1972	8	0.3	1.0
1975 Estimate B	19	0.5	2.2
1975 Estimate C	13	0.5	1.6
1978 Estimate B	21	1.0	2.6
1978 Estimate C	16	1.0	2.2

Sources: *Economic Trends*, February 1980, and information supplied by the CSO. The 1972 and the Estimate B data are from the *Economic Trends* article; the Estimate C data were supplied by the CSO in a telephone conversation in April 1980.

O'Higgins reached no firm conclusion from his calculations, merely stating that 'the magnitude of the hidden economy is a matter of faith rather than hard facts. Nevertheless . . . the effect of all the data taken together makes it difficult to believe a figure of less than 5 per cent, so that Sir William Pile's 7½ per cent is indeed "not implausible".'

The Feige report

Now for the latest and perhaps most thought-provoking evidence of all, that of Edgar Feige. When he turned his attention to the hidden economy in Britain, Feige used the same techniques which he had used in studying the United States economy, that is, the transactions method. To repeat, this is based on the assumption that a relatively stable relationship exists between the *volume* of non-financial transactions and the *income* produced by them. Reporting his findings in the *Journal of Economic Affairs* (July 1981), he argued that the total volume of non-financial transactions in the economy included monetary transactions in both the observed and the unobserved sectors, and that from them the total income which should have produced all these transactions could be determined. The difference, therefore, between the estimated total and the observed total provided him with his estimate of the unofficial economy, or unobserved income.

He obtained estimates of non-financial transactions by carefully examining the stock of currency in circulation, its velocity, and measures of the volume of cheque transactions for non-financial purposes. From these he concluded that the unobserved economy in Britain was approaching £28 million, fifteen per cent, or twice as much as the figure given by Sir William Pile. Feige admitted that his figures were only estimates, but asserted that they erred on the conservative side. In the same study, Feige also charged – unlike Macafee, for instance, who felt that it has been relatively static – that the unofficial economy had grown markedly in the 1970s. Taking the estimates of the unobserved sector as a percentage of official GNP in the period 1960 to 1979, he pointed out that the ratio of unobserved to observed activity appeared to peak in 1974 after rising in the first half of the 1970s. After that, it declined. These estimates, he suggested, showed that the massive recession and soaring inflation recorded in the official figures in the mid-1970s might be partly explicable in terms of a statistical illusion induced by the growth of the unobserved sector. Similarly, it follows, the fall in the rate of inflation in the latter half of the 1970s might also have been due to some falling off in the size of the unobserved sector.

Conclusion

So for every commentator and researcher we have a different figure for the size of the unofficial economy. What no one denies, however, is that it exists, and there are, therefore, implications for the British government in its taxation and social policy. It is not for us to suggest what the attitude to tax evasion should be, but the experience of the Italians, so long plagued by large-scale tax dodging, could repay study. James Ditton of Glasgow University, reporting to Inland Revenue workers in their staff magazine *Assessment* in September 1981, set out the Italian government's recent successful campaign against tax evaders in an economy where it has been estimated that at least thirty per cent of the whole economy was 'black' and, in some industries like clothing, seventy-five per cent of the industry was reckoned to be staffed by 'black' workers.

In 1979 the new Finance Minister, Signor Franco Reviglio, introduced a new way of dealing with the evaders. Instead of trying to catch every one of them, he found out who the main offenders were and went after them with highly public investigations. Surveys and spot checks were made and the selection of victims by computer was absolutely random. Evaders were publicly humiliated, their names and the amount of their evasion published in 'red books'. One evader was further 'punished' by the kidnapping of his child after his name had appeared in one of these books, leading other wealthy people to decide it was better to own up to their income and pay their taxes and so avoid the publicity which would have such a catastrophic result. That is most unlikely to happen in Britain, but Ditton suggests that 'a good dose of highly publicized randomness, together with the widespread publication of the names of the offenders' might be effective in the United Kingdom. In Italy, to conclude the story, the effect was swift and dramatic. In 1976, of the 2½ million non-PAYE taxpayers, it was reckoned that sixty per cent were declaring annual incomes of less than £5,400. One in six of them were declaring less than £900 and paying only £9 minimum tax a year. Between 1975 and 1980 Schedule D tax in Italy has increased from 22.7 per cent of total tax collected to 31.4 per cent.

The wine trade – easy for some

The painter and decorator we talked to was quite straightforward about how he ran his business. He certainly did not think he was being dishonest taking all the money he got from his part-time earnings. But what about others in actual recorded businesses, how do they return their earnings to the tax inspector? How do they fit into the unofficial economy?

We talked to a wine merchant, who felt that although things in the economy look bad, people still have a lot of money to spend, though they are not spending like they used to two or three years ago and margins are being squeezed.

'People have traded down a bit. A few are buying half-bottles where they used to buy whole ones, or are buying slightly cheaper, less good, wines. But they still seem to have plenty of money, despite what we read in the papers about unemployment rising all the time. Perhaps in a wine merchant's, you don't get many of those people – they'll go to the pub – but they say that people in white-collar and management jobs are becoming unemployed now. I don't know what the rate of unemployment is, but I don't imagine it leaves much room for things like beer, wines and spirits. I suppose quite a number of people are moonlighting and doing more than one job.'

'Yes. That's what we call the unofficial economy, where people either do two jobs, or work when they are registered unemployed, or run a cash business which they don't tell the Inland Revenue about. Do you think that happens at all in the wine trade?'

'It's almost certain to, isn't it? I imagine that in any cash business there is a little bit of fiddling at least, though on the whole I think any activity like that comes the other way – customers asking for special receipts and charging their wine bills to their company, as company and not personal entertainment. It's not up to us to question why they want receipts, written in a particular way, but this kind of thing seems to be quite widespread, especially in London. I doubt very much whether a great deal goes on in small towns. People there know too much about one another's business.'

'And you, how do you run your off-licence? Do you keep books correctly, or do you go in for a bit of money on the side yourself?'

'No. I don't think that that is the way to run a business. The tax we have to pay is not really unfair any more and after allowing all expenses I must say I'm quite prepared to pay my tax. Not everyone is, of course, and not everyone is as well established as I am. New companies often tend not to keep proper books. Then when the Inland Revenue start to take an interest in them, as they eventually do, because after all the off-licence is visible on the High Street, they either close down, or change their name and start a new company. That way, they can keep ahead of the tax man for years, though, of course, he catches up with them in the end.'

'So you don't involve yourself in the unofficial economy at all?'

'I don't think so, but I do have one or two reciprocal arrangements with people, if you include those. For instance, I don't pay for my dental treatment and my dentist doesn't pay for his wine, but do you think that is really dishonest? It's only a barter between two individuals and doesn't do anyone any harm. I do the same thing with my garage, though I have to pay something there, because the owner doesn't drink as much as my car costs in repairs! I'm sure a lot of business people have reciprocal arrangements like these. They are not putting anyone out of business and do ease our budgets a little. If we put bills in to one another, they would just balance out, so what's the difference? I get my dental treatment for nothing and the dentist gets the benefit of getting his wine free which has only cost me the wholesale and not the retail price.'

'But these things don't go through your books. What do you do about customs and excise duties and VAT?'

'Well, of course I can lose that in the books.'

'So in fact you are doctoring your books?'

'Only in a small way, nothing I think they would send me to gaol for.'

'You mentioned earlier that people seemed to have an enormous amount of money to spend still. Do you think that is what we call "black" money?'

'I imagine some of it must be. Buying wine is a good way of getting rid of money which you might have come by in a slightly dodgy way. It's not so obvious as buying things like cars and country cottages, but I imagine that not a lot of money is got rid of that way.'

'How much of your turnover would you say was "black" money?'

'Not a lot. Some people are able to put illegitimate expenses legitimately to their firms. Of course the firms don't intend that they buy drink with it, but how are they to know if the bill is doctored?'

'Do you find people buy for discounts and then resell illegally at higher prices?'

'Well, I don't know about illegally. Certainly, I offer discounts to people. Anyone who buys a crate of wine gets five per cent off and for people with big orders the discounts are bigger. But is there anything illegal in a restaurant buying wine from me and then selling at a higher price, if they put it in their books? Perhaps there isn't as much of this "black" business going on as people think. I do know, however, that some barmen or pub owners buy from me rather than the brewery, because my prices are lower. That way, they make more profit per bottle and it need not all show in the books.'

'Would you say that people have become more or less honest in their dealings in recent years?'

'I do believe that people try to pay as little tax as possible. It's only natural. I know that taxes have come down in recent years, but most of us think that they are still too high, so it's natural to try to avoid what we can. I admit it's easier for people like me to juggle the books, so that I pay less tax. But most people are employees and it's pretty difficult, if I remember correctly from my days as an employee, to evade pay-as-you-earn taxes.'

'Do you think the things you have said apply to other sorts of business?'

'Oh yes. I doubt if a grocer, for instance, pays for his food any more than I pay for my wine. There's a lot of barter goes on among small retailers, doctors, dentists, accountants and the like. Even my solicitor is not above taking a crate of wine for his services, rather than a cheque, and I know a doctor who hasn't bought a bottle of wine for thirty years – and he's not teetotal either! Some people simply pay in kind, and as well as picking up stuff from their own business, they can get effectively lower prices over a wide range of goods. But as I've said before, I think that's quite acceptable. These days business is bad enough without going out of your way to avoid some of the benefits of being self-employed. One would have to be stupid not to take advantage of unrecorded business deals.'

7 Politics and the unofficial economy

The connection between government policy and the unofficial economy can be discussed under two headings. First of all, the consequences the unofficial economy has for the economic and social policy of the government are of practical interest and importance. We will look primarily at the hard 'black' core of the unofficial economy, but also look at the larger area. There is also the question, which is also of great importance, of whether the government should have a policy on the unofficial economy, and, if so, what kind of policy.

The importance of the unofficial economy in government policy

Let us first assume that the government denies that there is an unofficial economy at all. Such an attitude is not unusual and is based on the assumption that its size and significance are negligible. In the light of what is going on, it is an assertion which cannot be maintained for long in good faith; after even the most superficial study it becomes clear that any government basing its actions on this belief is merely burying its head in the sand. Nevertheless, it was most governments' policy for a considerable time. The line of least resistance was followed and officially there was no policy for it at all.

Politicians and civil servants know that measures

against the unofficial economy are generally unpopular and best avoided for as long as possible. Only the tax man will object, and not because he has a greater concern for the common good, but from self-interest – it interferes with his work.

We must then ask ourselves what are the effects of such an ostrich policy, where governments acts as if there were no unofficial economy, on overall government policy?

An important aspect of the unofficial economy, as is clear from previous chapters, is that people generally have more purchasing power than is officially recorded. Does this have any implications for the incomes policy of our country? Let us assume, as the present British government does, that there is a need to moderate increases in incomes in the private and public sectors and to cut government spending. Newspapers daily carry reports of negotiations between employers and employees, or the government and civil service unions. What is odd about these is that the participants are often talking about basic wage rates and incomes. The participants negotiate seriously as if the area of negotiation is very limited indeed and as if many people are badly off. This is true in many respects, but is no reason why the negotiators should behave as if the unofficial economy did not exist.

By denying that the unofficial economy exists or severely underestimating its extent, the latitude in negotiating incomes policy is very narrow indeed. The government is depriving itself of one of the limited number of possibilities of reaching successful conclusions to negotiations. It is not admitting that individuals are better off in real terms than is officially revealed in the figures and general economic and social points of view. Were the government to replace this policy by one in which it tacitly or openly points out the 'black' core of the unofficial economy, then it would be in a much stronger position in wage negotiations.

This change would cause an uproar to begin with but it would not be long before most people fairly willingly accepted a substantial reduction in their unofficial income in return for their wage increases. When this tacit or 'blind-eye' policy is pursued, it is important to remember that many groups of people have little chance of getting any untaxed benefits at all. It was clear that the industrial action taken by British civil servants last year (1981) was partially caused by the fact that civil servants have much less opportunity of avoiding or evading taxes than other groups. Finding oneself in this position leads to frustration, which manifests itself to some extent in official discussions about the conditions of employment in the Civil Service. Frustration increases, because comparisons based on official figures may suggest that many civil servants are better off than their counterparts in the private sector: the reality is then all the more painful. It would probably be possible to remove or moderate the index-linked pensions of civil servants without overwhelming objections if it could be demonstrated clearly that index-linking feeds inflation. If the rate of inflation can be cut, real income will rise more substantially in the long run and bring better benefits, particularly if tacit reference is made to the hidden purchasing power. The trade unions would protest, but the protestations would have a hollow ring which would eventually be heard by the members.

What applies to the Civil Service can, of course, be seen in other parts of the economy and, although this is not yet clear to British workers, trade unions in some countries are now clearly opting for new job opportunities rather than massive wage increases. It should not be forgotten, too, that unofficial income makes employees financially more resistant in negotiations than they are officially supposed to be.

Now let us look at the labour market. As long as the unofficial economy is ignored in this area, government policy is directed at finding jobs for the unemployed, where official figures are now rising towards three million, as we write. The means chosen to solve this problem are mostly based on the Keynesian idea that unemployment can be reduced by raising government spending. The present British government has rejected this solution. Other methods used are designed to create employment for certain groups – say, the young, or those in particularly run-down areas. Such an employment policy is expensive in budget terms. As a result, the burden that the public sector puts on the economy is increased, either directly or indirectly, and the expansion of the unofficial economy is connected with the pressure exerted by the public sector.

Financing extra expenses by raising taxes and social contributions promotes redundancies. In fact, while this policy may reduce official unemployment, it will automatically increase hidden unemployment. If the head-in-the-sand policy is replaced by a 'blind-eye' policy, the government could take action in a more sophisticated and efficient way. On the one hand, it would then have to weigh up what the reduction in official unemployment costs in terms of the growth of hidden unemployment, and on the other hand a larger part of the budget could be directly allocated to its reduction. Furthermore, it would be realized that there are also secret jobs, which again make employment problems somewhat less acute than they are officially thought to be. It is even possible that the unofficial economy is so large that there is in effect full employment overall.

There are signs lately that the authorities in many countries are taking more account of the legal side of the unofficial economy. This gives an extra emphasis, for example, to the desire to moderate the growth of reported incomes for tax purposes. The time when people take the view that unemployment could be reduced by appointing dozens of different '. . . olo-gists' has gone for ever. In general, however, it is true that so far governments cannot or will not follow the 'blind-eye' policy and are officially refusing to take the 'black' part of the unofficial economy into account in a positive manner in taxation and social security policies.

This approach can also be seen in attitudes towards the money market. Whereas private banks in many parts of the world have for many years managed to channel the 'black' stream to the 'white' circuit in various ways, governments are behaving as if the existence of 'black' money has suddenly struck like a bolt from the blue. In the case of Holland, for example, the government reacted to savings certificates is-sued by the private banks in such a strong manner that individuals immediately cashed them and stopped putting their 'black' money in Dutch banks. This actually made the financial problems of the government even more acute, because it exerted an upward pressure on interest rates in the money market.

Governments are showing signs of taking into account the legal side of the unofficial economy somewhat more openly (each year, for example, the Inland Revenue now produces some estimates at its size in its annual report), but there is also a need for a systematic and coherent policy on the entire unofficial economy, including its 'black' core. The time has come, therefore, to examine this question in detail. The explicit or tacit denial should be replaced by an open recognition of the existence of the unofficial economy. We can no longer escape the need for a policy along these lines.

A policy for (or against) the unofficial economy

If one assumes an open recognition of the existence of the unofficial economy, the first question is whether the government should fight the unofficial economy, and if so, how. We now enter the field of political and social discussion, where value judgements are common. The question is no longer how things are, but how they ought to be. Political and ideological philosophies do not arise from scientific observations in an objective and logical manner but do indeed rest on value judgements.

For the sake of simplicity, we are assuming that, once the government has publicly recognized the existence of the unofficial economy, it will try to combat it. The way to do this is the subject of broad political discussions, where economic and social expectations once again play a decisive role. In those areas where the unofficial economy includes actions which break the law, combating them is a natural desire. Experience shows, however, that the way in which people react is not predictable, even in cases of law-breaking. Abortion on demand, euthenasia and squatting are all forbidden by the law, yet people are not always governed by the legal stipulations involved, and in the case of squatting, for example, it is positively condoned by the authorities and where there is a possibility of social unrest, the law is often ignored.

At this point, we must ask what the position of the 'black' core of the unofficial economy is. 'Black' transactions, which lead to 'black' money, are against the law, but rigorous official action against them also has serious economic and social disadvantages. Putting an end to the 'black' part of the unofficial economy at a single stroke would seriously damage production and employment. Our talks with people and the various indications of the size of the 'black' economy justify the conclusion that there would be a marked drop in the level of activities in commerce, building, hotels and restaurants and the medical field.

If one looks at the whole question in a moral and ethical way, it is relatively simple to balance the practice of the law to its application. The alternative – an economic approach to the law – has so far received very little attention in most countries. But when laws are looked at in this way they are judged not only from the point of view of whether they are just or not, but also for their effectiveness. The usual economic analysis is applied to them – alternative laws tend to be judged from two standpoints – their advantages and disadvantages are listed and evaluated with the aim of organizing and controlling society. This process puts an even greater emphasis on the justness and humaneness of any measures being considered. A simple example illustrates this fact.

Take a busy crossroads which is an accident black spot because the authorities have not installed traffic lights. Accidents would not occur, or would be far fewer, if traffic lights were put there. This means that the authorities are 'organizing' the road accidents to some degree. The logical thing for them to do is to install the lights, so that drivers do not have to rely only on their own and others' impeccable behaviour on the road. This analogy can be extended to society as a whole and the authorities can prevent or contribute to a great variety of casualties.

Now, another example to drive home the point. The cost of decoration and maintenance of one's own home is not tax-deductible, it is therefore in the interest of both house-owners and decorators to 'go black': the house-owner saves at least fifteen per cent by not paying VAT, while the decorator escapes income tax. Both people are breaking the law, and one's first reaction should be that they should be prosecuted and punished. This is easier said than done. It is not very easy to track down such transactions and anyway the situation is comparable to attempts to regulate the traffic at a busy crossroads merely by relying on people's behaviour and providing no traffic lights. Authorities organizing a society or community in this way pay the price when things go wrong. An alternative approach is to cease, so to speak, setting a fox to watch the geese. If the government made home maintenance costs tax-deductible, it would be in the house-owner's interest to enter into legal contracts, with proper bills and receipts. The next question is the level of financial advantage to be gained from the tax allowance: if it is more than VAT, then it is better to get receipts and send them to the tax man; if not, then the temptation to get jobs done without a receipt remains. Whether one gives in to this temptation depends partly on the risk of being discovered and partly on the penalty which follows. High tax rates, under-manning in the tax office, and relatively low fines for tax evasion tend to persuade people to take a chance on not being found out.

It is not our function here to set out ways in which the whole tax and social security systems could be reformed to cut back unofficial transactions, but it is imperative that governments should examine the return they get from the various rules and regulations. It is not enough simply to decide that certain actions will be legal and others not: it is just as important to know exactly what happens in reality and why. By using this approach, governments can begin to find effective measures to curb the unofficial economy. Measures which are permitted by law, but do not have the required effect, are ineffective – all that happens is that the goal recedes even further. As for Britain, the yields from certain taxes, as set out in Chapter 4, suggest that they are ineffective as revenue raisers and simply serve to encourage people to evade them.

When VAT inspectors, for instance, raid premises in cases of suspected evasion, there is generally a great deal of publicity, but the results are questionable and the offender often receives sympathy from the general public. Fines anyway are rare, proof is hard to establish and the net result very often is that the government is accused of running a police state in behaving in such a way over what people feel are minor transgressions. The same considerations apply to social security arrangements and for a realistic government approach, the starting point should be what things are, not simply what they ought to be.

We have argued that in order to combat the unofficial economy much more attention should be given to the effectiveness of the various possible measures than has been taken so far and this is also consistent with the need for a gradual and cautious approach towards reducing the rate of growth. Abrupt action would lead to enormous losses of jobs, production and incomes. Cutting public expenditure is also part of the gradual approach. There is no getting away from the fact that individuals on the whole would like to contribute less to the financing of the collective expenses of the nation than they pledge themselves to via Parliament. The public is dissatisfied – they get the impression that the government swallows up too large a part of their incomes, wastes their money and does not use it properly. The interviews contained in this book show that some people are prepared to avoid the official economy at any costs. Notwithstanding its annual audit, the government offers very little information about the way it spends its revenue and this lack simply feeds the unofficial economy.

As each successive Chancellor announces his Budget, accountants immediately work out ways of counteracting any measures which may increase taxes, particularly for the higher income groups. There is nothing illegal in these actions, but they have the effect of stimulating the lower income groups to measures which will increase their own effective income. Unless governments bear in mind this interaction between the 'black', 'grey' and 'white' parts of the unofficial economy, they will simply increase the frustrations felt by each section of the economy. Under the present Companies Act, directors of private companies can find various ways and means of increasing their incomes and, at the same time, avoiding personal losses in the event of their company's bankruptcy.

What we are suggesting is that there should be a

realistic approach to the political decision-making process: this is very different from the romantic idea of politics. We could illustrate the positive side of our approach to the whole field of politics, but it is necessary to restrict ourselves here to the unofficial economy.

As individuals, people like to dissociate themselves from the actions taken by the government for the benefit of society as a whole, indicating that Parliament does not actually do what the people want. It is not true, as is sometimes alleged, that the government serves the common interest of the people and that the private sector is governed by self-interest. The authorities are composed of individuals – politicians and civil servants – who act in a more or less coordinated way, but who nevertheless are still apt to be guided by subjective considerations. This means that there are no abstract objective authorities.

To show what really happens, we shall use what can be described as 'methodological individualism' to explain people's actions on the basis of individual behaviour and preference. In the case of the public sector, the behaviour of authorities is reduced to the subjective aims of politicians and civil servants. These are governed by self-interest rather than (and sometimes entirely instead of) the interests of the common good. Self-interest does not, of course, mean the acquisition of wealth, but individual aims that are determined by one's position.

Politicians, who depend for their elections on the goodwill of the public, never forget that the votes they will get at the next election depend on their current actions – the assumption that their decisions are designed to maximize their votes explains their actions rather than the assumption that they – the politicians – have the interest of the public at heart. Civil servants set much store by the size of the budget and staff allocated to them. Their behaviour can be explained by the desire to maximize their budget and their staff rather than simply by the desire to serve the common good. The term 'civil servant' is in fact misleading: they serve their own self-interests. In the private sector, self-interest is profit or growth, in the public sector, it means more votes, larger budgets or more power.

It is wrong to think that the public sector should take over control when the private sector appears to have failed: this view is based on the misconception that the authorities automatically and effectively act in the interests of the general public. In fact, there is often very little difference between the way the private and public sectors perform – one has to choose the lesser of two evils. It is only experience which reveals whether a function is better carried out by the private or by the public sector – it is impossible to predict this in advance.

Nor is it true to say that all that is needed to get socially acceptable results is to curb the behaviour of producers and consumers in the private sector. Transferring their activities to the public sector can easily give socially less than optimum results, because politicians and civil servants are just as much governed by self-interest as private individuals and decisions they take can be equally wrong. For example, civil servants can just as easily abuse their position of power in the same way as a company, if it has a monopoly of a particular product or service. The situation in both cases can be improved by competition.

The first conclusion from all this concerns the way collective pressure is put upon the government; it also helps to explain the appearance and growth of the unofficial economy. Members of Parliament vote for spending government money for this and that, because they can increase their own popularity in this way. What they are doing is buying votes for free. The higher taxes and social contributions which follow from increased government spending follow as a necessary evil. The burden is lowered on to the shoulders of the citizens as gently as possible, and it is sometimes suggested, for instance, that only people in high income groups should pay for higher government spending. This is not possible, however, as the reactions of some people show. When faced with a worsening of their financial situation some people simply sidestep the higher taxes by getting as much of their income in 'black' ways as possible.

Perhaps even more important is the realization that the unofficial economy is not confined to the private sector. The public sector is also a source of 'black' business. The risk situation in the public sector is of course higher than in the private sector, and it seems likely that there are fewer true 'black' transactions in the former. There is, however, no difference between the two sectors as far as the moral considerations involved are concerned.

This can be illustrated by considering the broader political problem of reducing the unofficial economy in general, and not just its 'black' part. This highlights what is the main problem for the 1980s – finding an acceptable ratio between the number of people in jobs and the number of unemployed. Many of the distortions of economic life today are connected with the increase in unemployment. As we have already seen, higher unemployment brings concealed production and jobs which do not figure in the official statistics. This means that reducing the level of unemployment and consequently limiting the growth of the unofficial economy should be central to government policy in the 1980s.

Before such a policy can be formulated and put into practice it is necessary to understand how unemployment arises. It is not just a matter of the swings and roundabouts of the world economy, but can be a result of deliberate government policy. It is facile to say that anyway unemployment no longer matters, as the government provides redundant people with social security payments, so that the worst excesses of poverty are avoided. The progress from potential to actual unemployment is fuelled by people who have to take economic decisions of one sort or another, and certainly not all of them are aimed at reducing government spending.

It happens in the private sector, too. Take a company which for one reason or another wishes to get rid of an employee, who perhaps has not been well for some time. It is cheaper for the company to get him declared unfit for work, rather than paying him out of its own sick fund. The company doctor will 'process' the medical data and the civil servants involved who will sanction the sickness benefit are most unlikely to find any reason to object. There is, therefore, facing the supply side of employment, a flexible demand side.

It is not unknown for governments to pursue policies which they know will bring an increase in unemployment. This may be quite deliberately associated with their aims for changing society and industry, say, cutting out overmanning, or attempting to limit the powers of trade unions. The greater the number of people seeking jobs, the looser will be the control trade union officials have over the shop floor.

Examples of this are becoming common in the United Kingdom: more and more workers are refusing to strike for fear of losing their jobs, or support fellow workers who may have unjustifiably been dismissed.

It is undoubtedly true that more people become unemployed than the ups and downs of the economy justify, because of government policy. Governments should take this into account when formulating their policies. A more objective assessment of the advantages and disadvantages of high unemployment is necessary than is often considered, simply because politicians often find it impossible to rise above their party policies for the sake of the common good. A study of the actual behaviour of people rather than an assumption of it, in whatever sector of the economy they work, can contribute to the development and implementation of a policy which is more effective than the present one.

Joel Barnett:
'You can't stop it altogether'

One man who has watched the unofficial economy grow since he first entered Parliament eighteen years ago is Joel Barnett MP, who was Chief Financial Secretary to the Treasury in the Labour administration of Mr James Callaghan. In the present Parliament, Mr Barnett is Chairman of the powerful House of Commons Public Accounts Committee. During 1981 the PAC has been taking evidence on the size of the unofficial economy and what can be done to combat it.

We asked Joel Barnett just how big he thought the unofficial economy was.

'Sir Laurence Airey, head of the Inland Revenue,

has put it around 7½ per cent of GNP,' he said. 'This estimate, which is the latest evidence we have, may rather understate the figure, because it includes only tax evasion. The problem about size is the lack of information. Nobody is going to say that they don't pay their taxes and risk being taken to court and facing severe penalties, including gaol.

'What we can do to get some guide is to look at actual expenditure figures and set them against official income to see what the gap is, but even that is not a particularly accurate guide, because there is expenditure which is not disclosed and not put through people's personal accounts or their business books. There is a clear tendency, I believe, where people think that they can get away with it, to understate income and overstate expenses.

'Where do you think the biggest abuses come?'

'There is no doubt in my mind that it is in businesses run on a cash basis, particularly small businesses. Once a business becomes anything like a decent size, it is extremely foolish not to keep proper books, because the tax inspectors will eventually catch up with the tax evader and legal action will follow. But a person running a small business can easily hide some turnover and profits. Take a person with up to half a dozen little shops: it's relatively easy to pocket the takings from one shop without the inspector getting suspicious. In a very small business, a fair amount of money is bound to go astray – it's only natural. In the fashion retail industry, say, gross margins are around fifty per cent. So a business taking £100,000 a year will have gross profits of around £50,000. After expenses that may be reduced to £25,000, but I imagine many such little companies in the fashion trade pay tax on only £10,000.

'In small retail shops in some other trades, margins have been cut to the bone by the competition from the big chains and it seems unlikely that people will survive. They work very long hours and would be far better off financially working for someone else rather than running their own business, but they like to be independent, so there must be some temptations for them to understate their income.'

'Small businessmen complain about being maltreated by the tax and social security systems. Do you agree?'

'That's nonsense. They just don't conduct their businesses properly. By not keeping proper books, they sometimes take money from their losses when they could in fact be getting tax rebates'.

'How do you think tax evasion could be stopped?'

'Where it lies makes it difficult to stop completely. It could be done if we had a gestapo-type of control over businesses, but I would not want to live in a society like that.'

'Would', we asked, 'lower levels of taxation help?'

'I don't think so. You know that a married man can now earn up to £14,000 a year and still only be paying tax at the standard rate of thirty per cent, though, of course, with national insurance contributions, the marginal rate goes up to thirty-six per cent. But even that is not high. I think that people's perception of the tax they pay is exaggerated. They think they are paying fifty per cent, when you have to have a very high income to do that. Relatively few people reach the high marginal rates and the very top rate is now only sixty per cent.

'I know that many businessmen blame their lack of success on tax, but that is just a fantasy excuse. After all, some businesses did very well in the Labour administration, in which I served, and marginal tax rates were much higher then.

'I do believe that we should have more highly qualified tax inspectors. There is certainly a shortage there, and where evasion is discovered, tough measures must be taken against the offender. We must stamp it down as much as possible. I won't pretend that we can stop tax evasion altogether. If people obviously live beyond their means, they must be investigated by the tax inspector. Constituents write to me and complain that the inspector has asked them this and that, but we cannot, as a society, tolerate blatant tax abuse. So-called "intolerable" levels of questions only arise when money appears to have gone astray. But in no case must we assume that just because things look odd that the person involved is automatically a tax evader.

'It is possible to keep quite considerable hidden earnings quiet. The banks, as you know, are under no obligation to tell the Revenue anything about an account holder, until there is a "black" money inquiry. Interest on deposit accounts eventually gets returned to the Inland Revenue, but if people are prepared to forgo their interest and keep "black" money in current account, it can be a long time, if never, before the tax man catches up with the evader. It's possible, too, to put money abroad in interest bearing accounts now that there is no exchange control. In law, such income must be disclosed by the British resident, but there is no requirement for the foreign bank to disclose the holding.

'On balance, I would put the size of the "black" economy somewhere between five and 7½ per cent and I do not think that the United Kingdom is particularly high in this respect. [The committee which

Mr Barnett was then chairing later suggested 7½ per cent.] People point to Italy, where everyone is alleged to be involved in some way with the "black" economy, but just look at France: it has to have very high levels of indirect tax, because the government simply can't collect the direct taxes it imposes. The French keep gold under the bed and evade their taxes, even though their net PAYE income is twice that of the United Kingdom. The "black" economy is a world problem.'

Conclusion

Our aim in this book has been to expose the distortions in our economic life, rather than to analyse the various legal and illegal activities which go on in our society. People tend to deceive themselves about these activities, and self-delusion leads eventually to delusion in society as a whole. The distortions are not limited to economic transactions. It is not infrequent for foreigners to marry British citizens without ever intending to live a normal married life; they simply want to be able to live and work in this country. In contrast, others with high incomes get divorced to save tax and then continue to live a married life. Children are born to parents who are officially divorced and unofficially married, officially unemployed and officially working, officially destitute and unofficially well-off. Little thought is given to these children, who barely know the difference between fact and fiction and are not taught to discern it.

The unofficial economy can no longer be called an occasional and negligible phenomenon. Our society is pervaded by it. People are withdrawing into their own private worlds, society is becoming more and more anti-social, the citizen is becoming alienated from the community, the call for solidarity remains unheeded, people distrust the authorities and any form of power in general, identification with the community is decreasing, and human contact is becoming grim and humourless. In such a climate, deceiving the authorities is seen less and less as an offence and more and more as a sign of skill and enterprising spirit. People used to be ashamed of tax evasion – now they are proud of it. Italians and Belgians are past masters in this field, but lost their monopoly some time ago. In every country there are developed forms of the unofficial economy and this inevitably has effects on other aspects of society. No country is more moral than any other in this respect; where tax burdens are similar, people's reaction will also be similar. The unofficial economy comes about and grows because people are discontented materially. They then refuse to take risks and want support from the authorities, yet at the same time they distrust and criticize them more and more.

The distortions in each country are aggravated by the international situation, where there is a lack of leadership and an increasing readiness to accept – or at least not to combat effectively – the use of terror for exerting pressure. The result is that individuals become even more nervous and more withdrawn, strengthening even more the unofficial economy.

'Black' money is only the tip of the iceberg, and the whole phenomenon deserves the attention of scholars, politicians and journalists. Knowledge and information are essential if there are to be improvements, or a complete solution, to the situation.

Index

Reference and Information

All these books are available at your local bookshop or newsagent, or can be ordered direct from the publisher. Indicate the number of copies required and fill in the form below

4

Name⎯⎯⎯⎯⎯⎯⎯⎯⎯⎯⎯⎯⎯⎯⎯⎯⎯⎯⎯⎯⎯⎯⎯⎯⎯
(block letters please)

Address⎯⎯⎯⎯⎯⎯⎯⎯⎯⎯⎯⎯⎯⎯⎯⎯⎯⎯⎯⎯⎯⎯⎯

Send to Pan Books (CS Department), Cavaye Place, London SW10 9PG
Please enclose remittance to the value of the cover price plus:
35p for the first book plus 15p per copy for each additional book ordered
to a maximum charge of £1.25 to cover postage and packing
Applicable only in the UK

While every effort is made to keep prices low, it is sometimes
necessary to increaes prices at short notice. Pan Books reserve
the right to show on covers and charge new retail prices which
may differ from those advertised in the text or elsewhere